YOUNG FIRST OFFENDERS:
THEIR CRIMINAL CAREERS

by

G. L. WEBB

Cover Drawing By: Chris Hedrick

Library of Congress Catalog
Card Number 78-72958

International Standard Book Number
0-933012-03-9

Printed in the United States of America

CONTENTS

		PAGE
INTRODUCTION		v
I.	THE DATA BASE	1
II.	THE CASE HISTORY METHOD IN CRIMINOLOGICAL RESEARCH	3
III.	YOUNG FIRST OFFENDERS	7
IV.	YOUNG FIRST OFFENDERS: THEIR CRIMINAL CAREERS (PART I)	11
V.	YOUNG FIRST OFFENDERS: THEIR CRIMINAL CAREERS (PART II)	117
VI.	YOUNG OFFENDERS — RECENT TRENDS	171
VII.	RECOMMENDATIONS FOR PREVENTION	175
VIII.	RECOMMENDATIONS FOR CONTROL	185

Introduction

The preparation of this manuscript was motivated by naive students and colleagues alike. Too often we view the world and human behavior as we think it should be or the way we would like for it to be, rather than the way it really is. This tendency appears to be most pronounced in the study of crime and criminals. So-called professionals (academicians) have traditionally and continually focused on the "poor unfortunate young people" who are victimized by our criminal justice system. We ignore the fact that there are a large number of brutal, irresponsible, manipulative individuals presently preying on the citizenry. I am afraid that young people studying criminology in our most prestigious universities are taught that the continued commission of brutal, predatory acts by offenders is, in large part, inevitable because of our "repressive capitalist system." Similarly, the mass media frequently presents offenders and ex-offenders as glamorous, exciting, and well-intentioned but perhaps misguided individuals.

In addition to the mass media's inaccurate and frequent romantic or sympathetic portrayals of offenders or ex-offenders, professional literature abounds with comparable inaccuracies. The tendency to present criminals (those incarcerated) as poor, unfortunate victims, suffering in prison because they were poor, black, politically active, or inaccurately labeled a criminal, is all too palpable. In fact, David M. Gordon (1975:42) argues that the biases of our police, courts, and prisons cause the relative violence of many crimes. He asserts that it is only natural that the criminals who run the highest risks of arrest and conviction may have to threaten or commit violence in order to protect themselves. Similarly, Gordon (1975:42) claims, "Many kinds of ghetto crimes generate violence, for instance, because the participants are severely prosecuted for their crimes and must try to protect themselves however they can."

Gordon (1975:45) views inmates as victims of a capitalist system, and asserts that our system of crime and punishment manages legitimately to neutralize potential opposition to the status quo by many of our most oppressed citizenry. He proclaims that, "the system" does this by perpetuating a set of institutions which feed large numbers of blacks (and poor whites) through the cycle of crime, imprisonment, parole and return to prison. He says "the system" locks up many for life and those "the system" occasionally releases are driven deeper into criminality by "the system." *The system*, according to Gordon (1975:45) keeps ex-offenders on the run "and unable, ultimately, to organize with others to change the institutions which pursue them." Finally, Gordon (1975:45) says "the system" blots the offenders' records with the stigma of criminality. Thus, "the system" effectively precludes the reform of even those criminals who vow to escape "the system," by denying them decent employment opportunities.

Eldridge Cleaver (1969:185) asserts that the parole system is a procedure devised primarily for the purpose of running people in and out of jail — most of them black — in order to create and maintain a lot of jobs for the white prison system. Similarly, George Jackson (1970) has written (while incarcerated in a state prison) that those black men born in the United States who are lucky enough to live past the age of eighteen are conditioned to accept prison as inevitable. Jackson (1970) also argues that once black men are trapped, the cycle (prison, parole, and the return to prison) continues almost independent of the will of those involved.

Susan Griffin (1975) argues that the problem is male socialization. In her article "Rape: The All-American Crime" she insists that males are taught to rape in our society. Griffin (1975:52) cites Professor Menachem Amir's Philadelphia study of rape and a parole officer in California to support her contention that rapists are normal, that is, normal within the context of our society. Griffin (1975:61) concludes her article in truly radical form by blaming the white male power structure for victimizing women, "raping" Vietnam, "raping" black people, and also "the very earth we live on."

The approach presented in this book cannot be considered radical or conservative. Simply a realistic approach, in that information is offered for the reader. Those who read this study will have an idea of the types of "mistakes" those incarcerated for three years or longer have made. The reader will be exposed to the criminal histories of numerous rapists, murderers, robbers, burglars, etc. Therefore, the reader will have a frame of reference from which to evaluate Susan Griffin's (1975:52) claim that rapists are normal, or David Gordon's claim that those incarcerated are victims of a capitalist system that severely prosecutes law breakers — so much so that, according to Gordon, many ghetto crimes generate violence because "participants" must try to protect themselves.

In the pages that follow, the reader will be exposed to the life histories (profiles) of inmates interviewed by the author during the years 1975 and 1976. The information presented in each case has been verified through official records. When information which has not been verified is presented, such information will be prefaced with such phrases as: "he states, he relates, he tells, he says, he indicates, he reports, he asserts, according to this inmate, etc." The comments attributed to inmates are statements they made to me during private interviews in my office. I have personally met every individual discussed in this manuscript and still correspond with some of them.

It will become apparent as one reads case after case that the factors most related to the imprisonment of an individual could hardly be described as race or poverty (poverty in the sense that some argue if the offender has money, he will not be incarcerated — race in the sense that some naively argue that many inmates are incarcerated because of the color of their skin not because they committed serious criminal offenses). I think it will become amply apparent that criminal behavior plays a key role in determining who is sentenced to prison.

This book may be viewed as an attempt to dislodge or at

least soften the axiom, "There is no substitute for experience." It is offered as a frame of reference to would-be discussants of young first offenders, crime, criminals, and the judicial system. It is expected that the careful reader of this text will have an understanding of criminal behavior, characteristic offense patterns, sentencing characteristics, and the administration of justice previously unavailable outside the realm of first hand experience. As long as academicians focus on the poor, unfortunate young man who was framed for armed robbery or burglary simply because he was black, his mother a whore, and his father a drunk — we should not be surprised at the unrealistic attitudes and views held by students of criminology. We need a realistic approach to the study of criminology, and that realism is what this book is about.

G. L. Webb

I
The Data Base

During my tenure (1974-1976) as a Correctional Sociologist in the classification unit of one of the largest (approximate inmate population 2600) and oldest (1877-present) maximum security prisons in the mid-west, I interviewed and wrote update classification reports on half (136) of those inmates who had been incarcerated in excess of three continuous years. The selection process was "random" in that the clerk in the unit non-systematically assigned half of the cases to this writer and the other half to a second sociologist. Thus, the selection process functioned to eliminate those inmates serving short prison sentences, i.e. less than three years. The selection process also eliminated from the study those inmates who had been paroled in less than three years, although their sentences were in excess of three years. Finally, serious offenders, who had served less than three years were also systematically eliminated from the study.

Constructing the life histories of inmates is made most difficult by frequent city, county, and state policies preventing the dissemination of juvenile criminal records. Such policies are motivated by professional arguments to the effect that once a young man or woman is labeled a delinquent, chances are they

1

will be treated as a delinquent. It is then argued that if they are treated as delinquents they will begin to view themselves as delinquents and act as delinquents. Thus, the best criminal histories available are extremely spotty. The FBI does not maintain FBI fact sheets for juveniles. Similarly many municipalities, counties, and states do not keep comprehensive records and frequently expunge juvenile records or destroy them when the offender reaches a certain age. Even those juvenile records that are not expunged or destroyed are frequently made inaccessible in an effort to protect the offenders' reputations.

Of the 136 original cases, 42 were selected for presentation because they either admitted to juvenile incarceration, or their records revealed that they had been incarcerated in one or more juvenile facilities; an additional 23 cases were selected for presentation because (in spite of the total lack of juvenile records in most of the cases) they represent some of the more comprehensive documented criminal case histories of young first offenders presently available.

The 65 case histories presented in this text are unavoidably spotty. However, they represent the best information available in an adult reception and classification unit. I personally constructed each case history presented by utilizing all the available information in each individual's master record file, coupled with a personal and private interview with each individual written about. The average interview lasted at least one and one-half hours. A few were as short as one hour. Many were two and three hours in length.

II
The Case History Method
In Criminology Research

A very obvious reason for the minimal use of the case-history method in criminological research is the fact that behavioral scientists are not willing to put in the time necessary to obtain and analyze such data. However a more basic reason for the scarcity of case-history methodology in the literature has been mentioned by Julian B. Roebuck (1978:84).

> Some of our colleagues are frustrated because some statisticians are much more interested in mathematical models than in research or research knowledge. And frequently, they confuse methods with the discipline of sociology. Sometime ago, a colleague said to me, "Sociology is numbers." The scary point here is not his account of sociology. We all give accounts. The scary point is that the fool believes that sociology is numbers. Most assuredly, he passes this on to others.

The case-history or what some researchers, such as Charles E. Frazier (1978) call the life-history method, is composed of a complete or some specified segment of a person's life. The case-

3

history method at its optimum level of validity is a carefully documented and verified biography constructed by a competent social scientist who understands the critical importance of verification and documentation. The case-history method at its lowest level of validity is simply an unchecked autobiography lacking documentation, verification, and social scientific scrutiny.

Sociologists have too frequently accepted the "own story" or autogiography of subjects under study. Many early sociologists were more concerned with achieving subjective understanding or the studied individual's definition of the situation than they were with constructing a carefully documented biography (see Shaw, 1930, 1931, 1938; Thomas and Thomas, 1928; Thomas and Znanieck, 1927; Sutherland, 1937). This is not to say that the case-history method is not abused or used inappropriately today. Although unchecked autobiographical data may be interesting, even intriguing, it should not be confused with quality research.

The approach voiced by David G. Morris as he wrote social histories of inmates received at a prison classification unit accentuates validity "If an inmate walks into your office dripping wet and tells you it's raining — look out the window." That is to say, if it is possible to check the validity of the information obtained from an individual or individuals studied, a conscientious researcher will check. The validity of the information obtained is quite obviously directly proportional to the researchers documentation efforts. When documentation is absent autobiographical data cannot seriously be viewed as evidence of real happenings.

In this regard, survey research should be criticized more than it is. Surveys of attitudes, values, and activities simply tell what the respondents say they believe and what they say they do. No attempt is made to check to see if the respondents do what they actually say they do.

Unfortunately the case-history method is also flawed by the absence of documentation efforts. Naive researchers too easily miss the most important methodological step, i.e., documentation. Even such out-spoken proponents of the case-history method as Charles Frazier frequently miss this most crucial point. For example, Frazier (1978:128) states, "The self-

4

perceived life-history method allows the researcher to identify the forces the subject felt, the way he or she felt them, the way he or she perceived others' feelings, and what modes of action followed.'' Frazier's assertion is in error! The self-perceived life-history method, like survey research, does not allow the researcher to identify the forces the subject felt, or the way he or she felt them, or the way he or she perceived others' feelings, or what modes of action followed. The self-perceived life-history method simply allows the researcher to identify in more detail than survey research the forces the subject *says* he felt, the way the subject *says* he or she felt them, the way the subject *says* he or she perceived others' feelings, and what modes of action the subject *says* followed.

Unchecked assertions by a respondent are simply statements lacking documentation and it is irresponsible for a researcher to elevate undocumented assertions to the level of fact or truth. Undocumented statements should be identified as such and prefaced with ''he or she states, tells, explains, asserts, claims, says,'' etc. to indicate the lack of documentation. For example, a responsible researcher should report a respondent's self-perceived life history as follows:

> When questioned regarding his health, this inmate stated, ''Good except for I lost my left eye (at a northern penitentiary) fighting.''

> During the interview, he stated, ''I get along with most people basically. I like a little group. I get along all right in the institution.''

> According to this inmate, he has always been a barber. He reports that he presently has an apprentice license and has eight months to go before receiving a registered barber's license. He says he is primarily interested in barbering.

> He states that he completed 11 years of school prior to incarceration. Although he has never completed a GED, he says he plans to get a GED and attend college after acquiring a registered barber's license.

> He explains that he has two brothers presently incarcerated at Mid-State Penitentiary. He states that he

5

has never been married. He reports fathering one child in 1968, but asserts that the child is now dead. He says he corresponds regularly with his mother, brothers, and sisters, who presently reside in-state. He reports that his father died in 1973.

Although we may sacrifice some literary merits by qualifying our information, it should be remembered that our primary goal is validity. If the information quoted above was not qualified with such statements as he states, he reports, he says, etc., and simply written up "as if" it were accurate, then validity becomes problematic. For example, when an inmate states "I get along with most people basically," or "I get along all right in the institution," the researcher should not assume truthfulness. If the researcher is genuinely concerned with how the respondent interacts with others in or out of an institution (penitentiary) he or she should check the inmates' "assumed to be true" statements. It may very well be, as in the above case, that attempted documentation will reveal that the respondent not only had a long history of anti-social activity in the free community but that he had also been transferred from a state boy's camp for "resisting supervision and pressuring his peers in camp." Further documentation efforts revealed a long history of anti-social activity as evidenced by numerous arrests for disorderly conduct, burglary, theft, purse snatching, fighting, and breaking and entering, as well as his incarceration in the past for incorrigibility, and most recently murder, armed robbery and attempted armed robbery. Therefore, the point to be made is quite obvious — interviews and self-perceived life-histories are not the most important elements in the case-study method, the most important element is documentation. Without documentation, the case-history method or what is sometimes referred to as the life-history method is simply a more indepth type of survey research whereby the respondents *say* what they believe, what they do, or what they have done.

III
Young First Offenders

The term "first offender" seems self-explanatory, but is it really? What is a first offender? Does the term "first offender" refer to an individual who violates the law for the first time, or does it refer to an individual who first commits a criminal act of such perceived seriousness that he is arrested for the first time; or does the term "first offender" refer to an individual who is not only arrested but charged with committing a crime for the first time, although he may have committed hundreds of crimes and been arrested on prior occasions but never formally charged; or does the term "first offender" refer to an individual who is convicted for the first time regardless of his criminal behavior, arrest record, or the number of prior occasions on which he was formally charged with offenses?

Perhaps the term "first offender" should be used to refer to those individuals without a prior conviction regardless of arrest records, station adjustments, or prior informal agreements resulting in the dismissal of criminal charges. If we define a first offender as an individual who is convicted of violating the law for the first time we can eliminate a certain amount of confusion, but we must further clarify our use of the term "first offender." When we say a "first offender" is an individual

7

who has been convicted for the first time, do we count traffic convictions; if not, should we count misdemeanor convictions, or should we just count felony convictions? A felony is defined by the new Merriam-Webster dictionary (1971) as "a serious crime punishable by a heavy sentence." Thus, how do we decide which convictions are serious and punishable by heavy sentences and which are not?

During my tenure as a correctional sociologist in the reception and classification unit of one of the largest penitentiaries in the United States, it was commonly accepted that any man sentenced to an adult penitentiary for the first time was a "first offender." That is to say, any individual who had not served a previous period of incarceration in an adult facility was labeled a "first offender." Even if an individual had been incarcerated on numerous occasions as a juvenile for offenses such as burglary, robbery, rape, kidnapping, aggravated assault, or manslaughter, he was considered a "first offender" when he was first received at an adult facility for committing additional offenses.

Such a definition of a first offender probably surprises most people, but it is a pretty common usage of the term "first offender." During my teaching experience I found that quite frequently students believed that a "first offender" or "first timer" in prison had only been arrested or convicted on one occasion, i.e., for the offense which led to his incarceration. Experience reveals quite the contrary however, the vast majority of first timers or "first offenders" have lengthy prior arrest and conviction records.

Contrary to the naivety often times expressed by academicians lacking any real experience, a prison sentence is not that easy to attain. The usual routine for young career offenders is:

1. Criminal behavior ⟶ verbal reprimands by police officers on the street (police discretion).

2. Continued criminal behavior ⟶ arrest, verbal reprimands by police (station adjustment).

8

3. Continued criminal behavior ⟶ convictions, judicial reprimands, small fines.

4. Continued criminal behavior ⟶ judicial reprimand, probation and/or suspended sentence.

5. Continued criminal behavior ⟶ violation of probation or conditions set by the court for a suspended sentence. The offender is then sent to a correctional facility, either juvenile or adult, depending on the offender's age at this point.

6. Release from a correctional facility, continued criminal behavior ⟶ parole violation and re-incarceration.

To demonstrate the usual routine described above, I have selected 65 case histories for presentation, i.e., 48% of the original sample.

IV
Young First Offenders:
Their Criminal Careers
(Part I)

Forty-two case histories (31% of the original sample) will be presented in this section. They were selected for presentation because the offender in each case either admitted to juvenile incarceration or his records revealed that he had been incarcerated in a juvenile correctional facility. The cases are arranged in chronological order, the youngest first. As of December 31, 1978, thirty-six (86%) of the offenders described below ranged in age from 22 to 35.

Case #401

Offense: **Sentence:**

Rape   7-21 Yrs.

Interviewed: 1976   **Birthdate:** 1956   **Race:** White

Most Recently Admitted to the Correctional Environment: 1973

Criminal History: This inmate plead guilty to the offense for which he is presently incarcerated. His records reveal that he stopped by a housing project, randomly selected an apartment, knocked on the door, and when a lady answered the door, he beat her, "tore up" her apartment, and forced her to leave with him. After leaving the housing project with the woman, he reportedly drove his car into a ditch and then he raped the woman. At one point during the sordid affair, this inmate apparently held the victim's head under water in a ditch because "she was screaming for help." This inmate stated that he was intoxicated at the time of the offense and that when he drank he lost control of himself.

This inmate first appeared in juvenile court in March of 1971, for breaking, entering, and stealing from a private home. He was placed on probation. In August of 1971, he was observed attempting to enter another private home. In September of 1971, he was placed under supervision of the Division of Welfare. He was subsequently placed in a foster home. However, his placement in the foster home did not prove to be beneficial. It was later learned that this inmate had dropped out of school and was described as very rebellious and abusive in school. He was also involved in numerous fights with other students at this time in his life and at one time a civil suit was being filed against him to recover medical and dental expenses. County records indicate that in December of 1972 after admitting to numerous felonies, including multiple breaking and entering, stealing, four automobile thefts, common assault, and sale of stolen merchandise, he was committed to a juvenile correctional facility. He escaped from the training school but later gave himself up to county authorities and was returned to the training school. He later escaped a second time from the training school and it was at this time that he committed the offense for which he is presently incarcerated. This inmate is presently listed as a runaway from a juvenile correctional facility for boys in an adjacent state.

When questioned regarding his use of alcohol, he stated that he only drank occasionally, but when he did drink he would get drunk. He does not report illegal drug usage.

Additional Social History: He does not report receiving vocational training prior to incarceration. Since incarcerated he explains that he has received a certificate for 2,000 hours in meat cutting and processing.

According to this inmate, he completed ten years of school prior to incarceration. He says he enrolled in the GED program in 1974 but quit because of a conflict with his job assignment.

He does not report ever having been married or fathering children. He states that his parents obtained a divorce when he was approximately 12 years old. He relates that he corresponds with both parents, his mother, who resides in-state, and his father in an adjacent state.

Case #402

Offense: **Sentence:**

Rape   7-20 Yrs.

Interviewed: 1976   **Birthdate:** 1955   **Race:** Black

Most Recently Admitted to the Correctional Environment: 1972

Criminal History: This inmate plead not guilty to the offense of rape for which he is incarcerated. He was first arrested in August of 1971, and charged with two counts of armed robbery (no

13

disposition shown). He was arrested and charged with burglary in October of 1971. He explains that he was sent to a juvenile correctional facility in 1971, at age 16, for committing the offense of burglary. Four months later, in the company of three others incarcerated for juvenile offenses, and while on a field trip in a National Forest Reserve, he and his companions raped a co-ed from a nearby university. In fact, this inmate and his accomplices took turns raping the young woman. Thus, this inmate was transferred to Mid-State Penitentiary at age 17 to begin serving his present sentence. When questioned during the interview regarding his plea of not guilty, he did not deny his involvement in the multiple rape and commented, "It's hard to believe it's real, but I know it's real." He states that he did not drink alcohol prior to incarceration, but indicated that he had used "acid" and "downers" on the street, stating, "I used to mess with that acid 'til it almost drove me crazy."

Additional Social History: During our discussion, he stated that he was wild when he was younger, and he now thinks that perhaps it was good that he was sent to prison. He says he "got it together" during a lengthy stay in "segregation." He comments that if he would have stayed on the streets, he would probably be dead now.

During the interview, he stated, "I can't stand nobody hollering at me or putting their hands on me." His records reveal that during the last 14 months, he has received numerous disciplinary tickets for fighting, possessing contraband, disobeying orders, disregarding orders, causing a disturbance, assault, insolence, and threatening a guard. This inmate relates that he joined the "Almighty Black Peace Stone Nation" while incarcerated in a juvenile correctional facility at age 16. He presently claims membership in the "Almighty Black Peace Stone Nation." He asserts that he intends to stop violating prison rules and says he would like to go to school and acquire a GED. During the interview, he was polite and cooperative.

He does not report having specific enemies at this or any other correctional facility in the State. He further indicates that he is not having unusual difficulties in adjusting to the correctional environment at the present time. He says he would like to be transferred to a Northern Maximum Security Prison because it's

14

"cool," and he's heard that you don't have to worry about any "unauthorized movement tickets."

When questioned regarding his acquisition of vocational skills, he stated, "I ain't had no vocational training." He expressed an interest in welding and electrical work.

According to this inmate, he completed eight years of school prior to incarceration. He states that he received additional education in a juvenile correctional facility and says he has been intermittently involved in the education program at Mid-State.

He reports that he has never been married or fathered children. He explains that he corresponds regularly with his mother and father who reside in-state.

When questioned regarding release plans, this inmate stated, "To tell you the truth man I don't know. I don't know what I plan to do."

Case #403

Offense: **Sentence:**

Burglary   1-10 Yrs.

Interviewed: 1976   **Birthdate:** 1954   **Race:** Black

Most Recently Admitted to the Correctional Environment: 1972

Criminal History: This inmate plead guilty to the offense for which he is presently incarcerated. He was paroled in May of 1973, and was arrested in August of 1973, and charged with disorderly conduct. Materials received from his parole officer reveal the following: At approximately 10:30 pm, one evening in August of 1973, this inmate called his parole officer and stated that he believed the City Police Department wanted him because of an incident earlier that evening at the home of his girlfriend. The victim stated that about 8 pm she was going to leave the house

to visit her aunt when this inmate stated she was not going to leave. When she tried to leave, he held her and hit her six or seven times in the face and tried to drag her into the bedroom. When she "got away and called the police," he left.
he left.

Later that same month he plead guilty to the charge of battery and entered a plea of guilty. He received a six month sentence. His records also reveal that he was bound over to the County Grand Jury on a charge of "illegal possession of a motor vehicle" in September of 1973. However, the charge was apparently dropped after this inmate was returned to Mid-State Penitentiary as a parole violator.

He states that he was sent to a juvenile correctional facility in 1969, but he denies knowing why he was incarcerated. His records indicate that he was sent to the juvenile facility in 1969 for assaulting and molesting a girl. It is further reported that he received a juvenile parole in April, 1970, and was returned to the facility in November of 1970 for "attempted auto theft and criminal damage to property." His records reveal that he was discharged from juvenile parole supervision three months after he received his present sentence for burglary and was incarcerated at Mid-State Penitentiary at the time.

His records indicate that he was arrested in 1971 for burglary; in May of 1972 for parole violation; and in June of 1972 for attempted rape, attempted armed robbery, and parole violation. During the interview, he stated that he had been arrested on numerous occasions as a juvenile but was evasive and uncooperative regarding the charges or disposition. When questioned regarding his use of alcohol, he stated, "I don't drink." He does not report using illegal drugs.

Additional Social History: During the interview, he described himself, stating, "I guess I'm like anybody else."

He explains that he had not received any vocational training prior to incarceration and states that he has not received any vocational training since incarcerated. When questioned regarding his primary occupational interest, he stated, "Hadn't really given it much thought."

According to this inmate, he completed seven years of school prior to incarceration. He reports receiving an 8th grade diploma at Mid-State in 1973. He says he was involved in the GED program in the past and that he took the preliminary GED test, failed it, and quit the program.

He states that he has never been married. However, he tells that he fathered two children and reports that the children presently reside with their mother. He comments that he and the mother of his children correspond "every once in a while."

During the interview, this inmate appeared lackadaisical, reflecting little if any motivation. He reports that he was involved in group counseling for approximately one and one-half months during the year 1975.

When questioned regarding his release plans, he stated, "I'll probably get married."

Case #404

Offense: **Sentence:**

Armed Robbery   8-15 Yrs.

Interviewed: 1976   **Birthdate:** 1954   **Race:** Black

Most Recently Admitted to the Correctional Environment: 1972

Criminal History: This inmate was convicted of armed robbery by a jury verdict. His records indicate that he and an accomplice robbed two men while armed with a knife and a pistol. This inmate was reportedly armed with the knife. Records indicate that his accomplice was shot and killed by the police when he (the accomplice) ran at the time of the arrest. He asserts that he is innocent of the charge for which he is presently incarcerated.

He had reached the age of 17 less than a week before he was arrested for the armed robbery described above. During the interview, he stated that he was first sent to a state juvenile correction facility at age 11 and that he was released from and

17

returned to juvenile facilities on numerous occasions until age 16 when he was sent to a state penitentiary. He claims that he has only been arrested for stealing or curfew violations. He says he was released from a juvenile correctional facility four or five months prior to his arrest for armed robbery in 1971.

His juvenile records reveal the following: In February of 1965, he was arrested for stabbing a youth in the back with an 8-inch butcher knife. In July of 1965 he was arrested for attacking a smaller boy with an ice pick. The local police indicated that there had been numerous complaints against the boy (this inmate) prior to 1965, but a comprehensive record had not been kept, due to the boy's youth. However, this inmate was reportedly involved in various fights, threatening teachers, purse snatchings, shop lifting, and "lying and cursing authorities." The juvenile division commented that he could give a most positive impression with his "yes sirs" and "no sirs." They also stated that he was the "biggest liar they had encountered." He describes his use of alcohol as "once a week" and does not report illegal drug usage.

Additional Social History: He explains that he was "hit in the head" with a pipe by another inmate in June of 1973. He states that he was blind for approximately three days after the incident and that he presently has problems with his vision. He says that occasionally things become blurry and he has to squint his eyes two or three times to bring whatever he is looking at back into focus. He also asserts that since the incident he has had occasional headaches which last two or three days. He relates that he does not know if his vision is 20/20 and that he has not had a recent eye exam, but he thinks one eye is weaker than the other.

During the interview, he stated:

> Most people say I'm quiet. Me myself, I'm like this, I don't look for trouble but I don't back down. I do my own time. I've done this bit myself. I always stay by myself and think. A lot of people say I've got a bad temper. Truthfully speaking, I get along better if I'm left alone. You come in, in the morning and

18

might say 'how are you'? and I might take it as an insult 'cause how can you be 'all right' in here looking at iron bars?

Throughout the interview he insisted that he was innocent of armed robbery and seemed quite upset because the parole board had not granted him parole earlier this month. He stated, "Half the people on the parole board are crazy." He argues that he is smarter than "a lot" of the guards (correctional officers) here and claims that he is harassed 24 hours a day. At one point, he said, "I'm amazed I ain't crazy after being here five years." He says most people wouldn't be able to endure "what he has" in the past five years.

When asked if he had any enemies at this institution or any other institution in the state, he commented, "No! I love them all! 'Cause I know what they're going through." He has a tendency to praise inmates in general and asserts that there are "a lot of innocent people" here (at Mid-State-Penitentiary) and "a lot of real intelligent people" incarcerated here that are so smart, "that they be talking and I don't even know what they're talking about."

His records indicate that he has been a "constant source of trouble" while incarcerated. He has received numerous disciplinary tickets which include the offense of fighting.

According to this inmate, he had not received any vocational training prior to his incarceration as a juvenile. He says he has received training in metal shops and wood shops since incarcerated. However, he states that he has not received any training at Mid-State-Penitentiary and asserts that he is not interested in "anything down here."

He reports completing ten years of school prior to his most recent incarceration. He tells that he has received "his education" in juvenile facilities. He claims to have received a G.E.D. in a correctional facility in 1969, and complains that his counselor wants him to get a G.E.D. at Mid-State-Penitentiary. During the interview, he revealed limited verbal ability and hand written materials included in his file reveal limited writing ability.

He explains that he has never been married but has fathered one child. He says the mother and child reside in-state, and that he corresponds with her regularly. He comments that his father died one year after his (this inmate's) birth and indicates that he

19

presently corresponds with his mother, brothers, and sisters who reside out-of-state.

He relates that when released, he plans to live with his mother.

Case #405

Offense:

Sentence:

Deviate Sexual Assault
Armed Robbery
Rape

6-20 Yrs.
6-20 Yrs.
6-20 Yrs.

(All sentences ordered to run concurrent)

Interviewed: 1976   **Birthdate:** 1954   **Race:** White

Most Recently Admitted to the Correctional Environment: 1973

Criminal History: This inmate plead not guilty to the offenses for which he is presently incarcerated. He was found guilty in a bench trial. The Official Statement of Facts reveals the following: one day in August of 1972 this inmate forced entry into the victim's home at about 7:00 a.m. He armed himself with a kitchen knife (10-inch blade), cut the telephone wires and entered the victim's bedroom. Armed with the knife he forced the victim to perform deviate sex acts several times and then finally raped the victim. He also forced the victim to write a check payable to him for $20.00. After keeping the victim at knife point for approximately three hours, he left the premises. He was subsequently extradited from Oklahoma and charged with the above offenses. Regarding the offenses for which he is presently incarcerated, he stated that he did not know what happened because he "didn't listen to that shit they said in the court room."

This inmate asserts that he was arrested approximately 10 to

20

15 times as a juvenile. He says he was sent to a juvenile correctional facility at approximately age 13 for running away from home. He relates that he was released approximately six months later, although he was returned to a juvenile facility at approximately age 15 for running away from home and auto theft. His records indicate that he was arrested for burglary investigation in 1970 (no disposition shown); theft in February of 1972 (victim refused to sign complaint when property was returned); and later the same year he was arrested for possession of marijuana, contributing to the delinquency of a minor, possession of alcohol, and burglary (no convictions noted). He states that he only drinks alcohol on weekends and does not report illegal drug usage.

Additional Social History: During the interview, this inmate stated, "Sometimes I'm easy to get along with, sometimes I'm not." When questioned regarding possible motivation for past criminal activity, he stated, "Just done it cause I felt like doing it. I got tired of people telling me not to."

He does not report having specific enemies at this or any other correctional facility. He seems to take pride in the fact that he has received numerous disciplinary reports while incarcerated. When asked why he had not received a disciplinary ticket in recent months, he stated, "They decided to stop fuckin' with me because they know I'm not going to pay any attention to them." He further commented, "They've got me on the 'pay no mind' list, where if I tell them off they don't pay any attention."

This inmate does not report receiving any vocational training prior to or since incarcerated. His records indicate that during the last eight months he has spent three months in segregation and the other five months on an unassigned gallery. He explains that he is presently the clerk on 10 Gallery, East House (unassigned). He asserts that he is primarily interested in "nothing" as far as occupations are concerned.

According to this inmate, he completed eight years of school prior to incarceration. He states that he has not been involved in any educational program since incarcerated. He says he is not interested in acquiring a GED and commented, "I haven't got the patience for that shit."

He does not report ever having been married or fathering

21

children. He relates that his mother and father were divorced immediately after he was born. He tells that his mother remarried when he was four years old. He says he telephones his mother once a month and that he has not communicated with his father since 1970.

This inmate relates that he plans to work for his step-father when released although he asserts that he and his step-father have never "got along very well." He also insists that he will be making $10 an hour while working for his step-father.

Case #406

Offense: **Sentence:**

Deviate Sexual Assault	12-35 Yrs.
Deviate Sexual Assault	12-35 Yrs.
Deviate Sexual Assault	12-35 Yrs.
Armed Robbery	12-35 Yrs.
Armed Robbery	12-35 Yrs.
Armed Robbery	12-35 Yrs.

(All sentences ordered to run concurrent)

Interviewed: 1976   **Birthdate:** 1954   **Race:** White

Most Recently Admitted to the Correctional Environment: 1973

Criminal History: This inmate plead guilty to the offenses for which he is presently incarcerated. He was originally charged with three counts of armed robbery, three counts of indecent liberties with child, and six counts of deviate sexual assault. His records indicate the following: This inmate, while armed with a knife, robbed three young men, forced each of the young men to fellate his penis, and he (this inmate) then fellated each of the victims' penises.

22

He states that he was first arrested at age nine for drinking, being disorderly, and assault with a deadly weapon. He commented, "I got drunk and a cop tried to take me out of a bar and I didn't like the way he put his hands on me when he tried to take me out of the bar so I just turned around and cut him."

This inmate brags that he was arrested nine times in one month at age nine for being drunk and disorderly. He says he was arrested twice at age 11 for driving without a driver's license. He relates that he was arrested at age 14 for "hit and run driving."

He tells that he was sent to a juvenile correctional facility at age 15 for deviate sexual assault, but he asserts that he was not guilty. According to this inmate, he was released from state juvenile facilities approximately eleven months later. However, he says he was committed to a juvenile facility at age 17 for living with an older woman, drunken driving, and being in possession of stolen credit cards.

He states that he escaped from a state juvenile facility at age 18 and was arrested a short time later for rape. He says the charge of rape was dropped and he was sent to another juvenile correction center at age 18. He says he was released on juvenile parole approximately four months later and he asserts that he was arrested for the present offenses 20 days later.

His records indicate that he was arrested and fined for being a minor in possession of liquor in February of 1970. He was charged with three counts of deviate sexual assault in June of 1970 and was sent to the Department of Corrections (juvenile division). He was arrested for theft in July of 1972 (which was dismissed when he received a sentence of 35 days for escape). His records also indicate that he was paroled in January of 1973 (42 days prior to his arrest for the present offense), and was on parole when arrested for the present offenses.

When questioned regarding his use of alcohol, he boasted that he drank half a case of Budweiser and three bottles of Seagram's Seven per day. When questioned regarding illegal drug usage in the past, he stated that he had never used illegal drugs. However, a psychiatric report written in 1973 reveals that this inmate was "out on a day's program" and bought

23

Darvon, Seconal, and nine bottles of Seagram's Seven whiskey, taking them back to the Reception and Diagnostic Center, drinking and getting in a fight with one of the guards. Said report also refers to this inmate as a drug abuser (cocaine, amphetamines, and barbiturates).

Additional Social History: His records reveal the following: This inmate had lived with his maternal grandmother since infancy. He was an only child. However, he has three half-siblings. His parents were divorced in 1955. He has presented behavioral problems as far back as 1965. A school report dated in January of 1965 described him as lacking inner control and being unwilling to accept the external controls necessary to adjust to the everyday requirements of interpersonal relationships and, on some occasions, he had terrorized his classmates and intimidated his teachers. In May of 1965 a county court adjudicated him a dependent child and he was placed in the guardianship of the Department of Public Aid. In June of 1965 he was placed in the Midwest Children's Center in an adjacent state where he remained until May of 1966. While there, he was a constant trouble-maker outside the classroom and required constant disciplinary action. His play attitudes tended to be very destructive, even dangerous in competitive games. He was also described as having failed to establish appropriate controls over impulsive behavior. Consequently he needed intensive and extensive supervision.

In May of 1966 he returned to the same state in which Mid-State Penitentiary is located to again live with his maternal grandmother. In October of that year, a school psychologist recommended that he be placed in a residential treatment center for emotionally disturbed children. In May of 1967 he ran away from home and when apprehended refused to return to his home. He was placed in a youth home in May of 1967 and three days later he was placed in a ward for emotionally disturbed adolescents inside a state hospital. At first he exhibited the same kind of uncontrollable behavior but eventually he became quieter and more cooperative and began to get along better with others. Home visits were initiated and they seemed to go well. He was released from the hospital in July of 1968 and once again went to his grandmother's home.

24

In March of 1969 he was again placed in a state hospital (pyschiatric ward) and twelve days later he was placed in an Achievement Center in the State of Texas. He remained there until he fled in January of 1970.

A psychiatric report written in October of 1973 relates that this inmate is not mentally deficient. He represents an antisocial personality with emotionally unstable features with alcohol and drug abuse (Cocaine, amphetamines, and barbiturates). He is explosive at times; unpredictable, impulsive and non-reflective. This inmate's exaggerated and grandiose ideas of his talents and abilities reflect his extreme lowered self-image and self-esteem. This inmate's hostility toward his parents is obvious. He sorely lacked supervision and guidance in his formative years.

When questioned regarding his behavioral history, this inmate stated, "I ain't got nothing else better to do. What I'd like to know is why everybody is so concerned about crimes?" He described his personality stating, "I would describe myself as a person when I want to be." He asserts that he was a member of a street gang by the name of "The Outlaws." He says he started committing crimes when he joined the "Black Hands" at age 15. However, as noted earlier, he reports criminal behavior at least six years prior to age 15.

When asked if he had specific enemies at this or any other correctional facility in the state, he stated, "Here I have about 500 enemies and they're all gang members." He claims to be an expert on explosives and says the "Stones" wanted him to aid them with his knowledge of explosives but he refused. He insists, "No program in this joint interests me."

He claims that he received training in the area of explosives in North Carolina on a Cherokee Indian Reservation. He also claims to have experience in the area of auto mechanics (which he says he received in North Carolina, California, Missouri, Texas, and Mississippi). He states that he is primarily interested in carnivals as an occupation.

According to this inmate he completed one year of school prior to incarceration. He asserts that he was "thrown out" of second grade for raping the school teacher. He says he did not rape her, and he insists that she grabbed him around the neck so he ripped her dress off. In addition he stated, "Besides that, she was a black school teacher. If she'd been white I wouldn't have done nothing.''

He states that he was married in 1973 and says he presently remains married. He tells that two children (twin girls) resulted from the union. He relates that the children presently reside with his wife on a Cherokee reservation located out-of-state.

When questioned regarding release plans, this inmate stated that he plans to open a carnival the third day he is out. He claims that he and a partner of his already have all of the equipment necessary. He says he plans on being "out" a month before he goes to the parole board.

Case #407

Offense: **Sentence:**

Armed Robbery   5-8 Yrs.
Attempted Rape   2-6 Yrs.

(Sentences ordered to run concurrent)

Interviewed: 1976   **Birthdate:** 1953   **Race:** Black

Most Recently Admitted to the Correctional Environment: 1973

Criminal History: This inmate plead not guilty to the offenses for which he is presently incarcerated. He was convicted in a bench trial. His records reveal that at approximately 6:10 pm one day in January of 1973, this inmate and two accomplices robbed a woman, stripped her to the waist, and attempted to rape her. The rape attempt was halted when the victim's brother-in-law appeared in the hallway where the offenses were taking place. It is further reported that a shot was fired at the brother-in-law as this inmate and his accomplices fled the scene.

He explains that he was first arrested at approximately age

26

ten for burglary and was subsequently sent to a juvenile facility for approximately nine months. He relates that he was arrested a second time at age 13 for theft and was again sent to a juvenile facility for approximately ten months. He states that he was arrested a third time at age 13 for burglary and was again returned to a juvenile facility for approximately 15 months. He was arrested at age 16 for investigation of burglary — then released. At age 17 he received a two year sentence for burglary which he served in an out-of-state penitentiary. He was paroled January 3, 1972. It is suspected that this inmate was still on parole when arrested for the present offenses.

When questioned regarding the offenses for which he is presently incarcerated, this inmate asserted that he was not guilty and that he had never seen the victim before in his life. When questioned regarding his use of alcohol, he stated, "I don't drink at all." He does not report illegal drug usage other than marijuana.

Additional Social History: He describes himself as "friendly and quiet." He insists that the reason he has been in so much trouble is he wasn't treated right when he was a "little boy." He asserts that he was not treated like everyone else. In reviewing psychiatric evaluations included in this inmate's file, it is noted that since 1975 he has had the following drugs prescribed for him: Librium, Valium, and Mellaril. His records indicate that he is presently taking Mellaril only. It is further noted that in April of 1975, this inmate informed the staff psychiatrist that he wanted to see somebody associated with the Cancer Association because he knew the cure for cancer. When asked how he obtained the cure for cancer, he stated that he had attended church and listened to a sermon by a preacher he trusted very much. Later that night, he dreamed about the sermon and he discovered the cure for cancer.

He reports receiving welding and upholstery training prior to incarceration. He also asserts that he knows the body and fender repair business very well. However, he does not report receiving any vocational training "to speak of" since incarcerated. He states that he is primarily interested in auto body and fender repair and becoming a creative communications director.

According to this inmate, he completed eight years of school prior to incarceration. He explains that he has never pursued a GED in spite of the fact that he has been incarcerated on numerous occasions. He says he thinks he is all right when it comes to education, commenting, "I studies a lot."

He does not report having been married or fathering children. He states that he was born and reared out-of-state. He relates that his mother and father were never married, nor did they ever live together to his knowledge. He reports that his parents presently live out-of-state and that he corresponds with his mother only.

He states that he was involved in career counseling for approximately two months earlier this year. He states that he is not interested in group counseling because he does not need a counselor; he insists that he can get anything he wants inside the prison with cigarettes.

When questioned regarding release plans, he stated that he planned to travel to the capital. When questioned regarding his expressed desire to travel to the capital, he stated because of "a girl there I'd like to have."

Case #408

Offense: **Sentence:**

Murder   14-18 Yrs.
Attempted Robbery   2-7 Yrs.

(Sentences ordered to run concurrent)

Interviewed: 1976   **Birthdate:** 1953   **Race:** Black

Most Recently Admitted to the Correctional Environment: 1972

Criminal History: This inmate plead guilty to the offense for

28

which he is presently incarcerated. In October of 1972, he received a two to seven year sentence for Attempted Robbery. His records reveal the following: This inmate and an accomplice attacked the victim on a darkened sidewalk and attempted to knock him down and take his property.

In November of 1972, this inmate received a fourteen to eighteen year sentence for Murder. His records indicate the following: This inmate attacked the victim in her backyard, knocked her to the ground, pounded and stomped on her, pulled down her pants, looked for money, and attempted to sexually molest her. He fled from the scene without finding any money. The victim suffered several lacerations and a fractured skull. The victim died three days later. Local county officials assert that this inmate is a dangerous person and investigations (conducted in 1972) linked him to fifteen other robberies in the committing county.

This inmate explains that he was sent to a juvenile correctional facility at age fourteen for aggravated battery and robbery. He says he was released on juvenile parole at age fifteen. He was arrested and charged with "possession of a controlled substance" in July of 1972 (no disposition shown). He describes his use of alcohol as "very light" but does admit to using illegal drugs in the past such as "speed," "acid," and mescaline. He does not report ever having been addicted to illegal drugs and he asserts that he has never had a "habit."

Additional Social History: He explains that he received experience as a short-order cook prior to incarcertion. He states that he received a certificate in heavy equipment operation in 1974, but asserts that he has never operated a piece of heavy equipment, and has no experience other than reading a book about heavy equipment. He indicates that he is primarily interested in cooking, masonry, and business management.

This inmate reports completing nine years of school prior to incarceration. He relates that he received a GED at Mid-State Penitentiary in 1974. He has expressed an interest in college vocational courses in the area of business management.

He does not report ever marrying or fathering children. He states that his mother died in 1975. He says he corresponds regularly with his father and brothers who presently reside in-state.

When released he says he plans to pursue the occupational area of business management.

===

Case #409

Offense: **Sentence:**

Murder   75-90 Yrs.
Deviate Sexual Assault   13-14 Yrs.

(Sentences ordered to run concurrent)

Interviewed: 1976   **Birthdate:** 1953   **Race:** White

Most Recently Admitted to the Correctional Environment: 1969

Criminal History: This inmate plead guilty to the offenses for which he is presently incarcerated. His records reveal the following: In 1968 the victim of the offenses was walking home from high school when this inmate, (then 15 years old) and an accomplice approached the boy (the victim) and tried to sell him a transistor radio (which this inmate and his accomplice had obtained earlier that day in a burglary). When the victim refused to buy the radio, this inmate and his accomplice began to push and hit him. They then pushed and drug the victim into a vacant lot adjacent to the street, which was covered by high brush and weeds. While in the lot, this inmate and his accomplice forced the victim to suck their penises and submit to anal intercourse. A record of this inmate's version of the incident reveals that his accomplice had anal intercourse with the victim while the victim was forced to suck his (this inmate's) penis. It is also reported that positions were then reversed and this inmate had anal intercourse with the victim while he (the victim) was then forced to suck the accomplice's penis. The state's attorney relates that after these acts were completed, the

30

victim was beaten by this inmate and his accomplice with their fists, kicked with their feet, and beaten about the head with a metal bar and concrete block. The immediate cause of the victim's death was brain damage due to the beating.

This inmate explains that he and his accomplice plead guilty to the offenses and that they had been drinking beer and sniffing glue prior to the offenses. He reports that he, his accomplice, and the victim were fifteen years old at the time. He also states that he had been arrested approximately three times prior to committing the offense for which he is presently incarcerated. He says he was arrested for running away from home, breaking out windows, and breaking and entering at age fourteen for which he received six months probation. He further relates that he was on probation when he and his accomplice committed the murder and deviate sexual assault. He does not report using illegal drugs, although as noted above, he does report sniffing glue.

Additional Social History: During our discussion, this inmate made reference to himself prior to incarceration stating, "back then, I was a show-off and tried to do things to make people look at me, like stealing and getting into trouble, exciting things." He relates that he used to do "those things" to get friends. Now he says he no longer shows-off and he says he has a few associates in the penitentiary, "but not really friends 'cause the guys in here just want to use you."

During the interview, he appeared intellectually slow, spoke slowly and simply, and stuttered on occasion. He is small in stature and rather boyish looking.

He does not report having specific enemies at this or any other correctional facility in the state. However, he says there are a number of people here that he tries to stay away from because "a lot of them" want him "to act like a girl for them," or sell drugs, or get involved in some "racial stuff."

Since incarceration, he reports receiving training in the areas of auto mechanics, auto body repair, and welding. He states that he has also received vocational experience as a mechanic on the knitting machines at Mid-State, as well as clerical experience while working as a clerk and runner. Although he reports receiving the above-mentioned experience

31

and training, he says he has never received a training certificate. He does not report having any specific vocational interests.

According to this inmate, he had just started eighth grade when he was arrested for the offenses for which he is presently incarcerated. He states that he received an eighth grade diploma at a juvenile correctional facility for boys in approximately 1970. He relates that after leaving the juvenile facility and arriving at Mid-State Penitentiary at age eighteen, he studied for the GED and took the exam on two different occasions. Although he reports failing the GED exam twice, he says he "might try it again."

He states that he has never been married or fathered children. He indicates that his mother and father presently reside in-state, and they (he and his parents) correspond regularly. He also commented that his parents visit him as often as they can (three times a month).

When asked about his release plans, he said he has always wanted to be a policeman or a soldier.

Case #410

Offense: **Sentence:**

Indecent Liberties w/Child   4-8 Yrs.

Interviewed: 1976   **Birthdate:** 1952   **Race:** White

Most Recently Admitted to the Correctional Environment: 1973

Criminal History: This inmate plead guilty to the offense for which he is presently incarcerated. The Official Statement of Facts reveals the following: one day in July of 1973, at approximately 11:00 a.m., this inmate forced his niece (age 10) to perform an act of oral copulation upon him. The defendant then inserted his penis into the victim's rectum. These sexual acts were witnessed by the victim's sister (age 7) while they were occurring in the bedroom where this inmate resided.

He reports that he was first arrested at age 16 for running away from an orphanage. He further reports that he was subsequently sent to a juvenile correctional facility for approximately six months. He says he was arrested a second time at age 18 for two counts of burglary, and received a five year suspended sentence; he asserts that he was also told to leave the State of Georgia. He relates that he was arrested a third time for five counts of grand larceny at age 18. He says he served six months in an Army stockade before the charges were dropped. According to this inmate he was arrested a fourth time in November of 1971 for attempted burglary, and then released. His records reveal that he was arrested for disorderly conduct in May of 1972 (no disposition shown). He was arrested in September of 1972 for attempted burglary which was reduced to attempted theft and he received one year probation. Thus, this inmate was on probation when arrested for the present offense. In addition to the above, he was arrested twice in 1973 on charges of being a "peeping Tom." He does not report using alcohol or illegal drugs.

Additional Social History: He describes himself prior to incarceration as, "a very stupid unlearning punk." He commented, "I never took the time to think. I never took the time to look at the consequences." He also stated, "I try to play Mr. Nice Guy too much." He asserts that on occasion he has been known to have a very bad temper, but says he cannot hold a grudge. When questioned about sexual activity prior to incarceration, he related that his "sex life was minimal in the past."

A psychiatric evaluation written in January of 1974 relates the following: He is probably of low normal intelligence. Inadequate personality with anti-social features. This inmate is immature and has a poor self-image resulting in poor heterosexual adjustment and anti-social behavior.

A psychiatric evaluation written in April of 1975 reports that this inmate lives on the pleasure principal, is impulsive, and does not anticipate the consequences of his behavior. He has not shown any special propensity to aggression. He has no ambitions and has developed no special skills. The sexual act involved was more experimental than anything else. It does not have the quality of force or harm intended nor irresistable impulse. He has a somewhat perverse curiousity about sexual matters and lacks judgment in acting on these.

He does not report having specific enemies at this or any other correctional facility. He further indicates that he is not having unusual difficulties adjusting to the correctional environment at the present time.

This inmate states that he received training as a combat medic during his enlistment in the Army in 1970 and 1971. He also states that he has received training in the area of ceramics for approximately 14 months at Mid-State.

According to this inmate, he completed ten years of school prior to incarceration. He relates that he received a GED at Mid-State in 1975. He states that he is presently enrolled in college and has completed 30 college semester hours as of this date.

He does not report ever having been married or fathering children. He tells that this mother died in 1966 and that he has not seen his father since age five. He says he corresponds with his older married sister who resides in-state.

Case #411

Offense: **Sentence:**

Attempted Murder	15-45 Yrs.
Attempted Murder	15-45 Yrs.
Attempted Murder	15-45 Yrs.
Rape	15-45 Yrs.
Indecent Liberties with a Child	15-45 Yrs.

(All sentences ordered to run concurrent)

Interviewed: 1976   **Birthdate:** 1952   **Race:** White

Most Recently Admitted to the Correctional Environment: 1973

Criminal History: This inmate brutally beat two young girls, one age three and the other age five. The girls were found in the basement of their home. The three year old girl had been sexually assaulted and this inmate plead guilty to having sexual intercourse with the child. In addition, this inmate had shoved a wooden stick into and through the three year old's vagina, lodging it (the stick) in the child's abdomen. The stick was approximately 20 centimeters in length and over two centimeters in width. The stick had to be surgically removed. This inmate plead guilty to three counts of attempted murder in connection with the severe nature of the beatings, and the insertion of the wooden stick (the stick appeared to be a bed rail from a baby crib) into the three year old's vagina. He also plead guilty to raping and performing an act of lewd fondling or touching of the three year old victim.

His records indicate that as a child, he set fire to the parental home. In 1967 he was committed to a juvenile correctional facility as a delinquent charged with being a runaway, shoplifting and auto larceny. In 1968, he was charged with "sex involvement." He explained that he was messing with boys, but asserts "it wasn't anything." He was paroled in 1968 and was returned in 1969 for vandalism and wrecking two tractors which he took without permission.

He tells that he has been arrested on numerous occasions for offenses related to alcohol. He reports that he joined the Army in 1971 and received an undesirable discharge in 1972 after being arrested for possession of a stolen automobile, being absent without leave, and violation of the Dyer Act. When questioned regarding his use of alcohol, he stated that he drank every day, but socially. He reports using illegal drugs, what he refers to as "light stuff", primarily marijuana and "speed."

Additional Social History: His records report the following: He was enuretic until the age of 14. He peeped in windows for "something to do." He used to drown cats and throw them against walls. He denies exhibitionism and denies homosexuality. He denies any previous sexually deviant acts with children. He does not show any particular remorse for

35

committing the offenses for which he is presently incarcerated.

During the interview, this inmate stated, "I try to get everybody to like me because I'm easy going and fun to be with, but I wouldn't really trust no one."

He reports that he has enemies at Mid-State Penitentiary because of the nature of the offenses for which he is presently incarcerated. However, he does not report having specific enemies at this or any other correctional facility in the state. He further indicates that he is not having unusual difficulties in adjusting to the correctional environment at the present time.

He reports receiving "a little training" in the areas of auto mechanics and farming prior to incarceration. He states that he also worked as a caretaker in a graveyard. He does not report receiving any vocational training "to speak of" since incarcerated.

According to this inmate, he completed eight years of school prior to incarceration. He has not acquired a GED nor is he presently involved in an educational program.

He does not report ever having been married or fathering children. He says he hasn't written his parents in approximately one year, stating, "I cut 'em off." He states that his mother and father presently reside in-state. He relates that he presently corresponds with "some broad over in (an adjacent state)."

He states that he is not interested in group counseling, commenting, "I don't think I could handle it."

Case #412

Offense: **Sentence:**

Burglary   2-6 Yrs.
Escape   (consecutive) 1-2 Yrs.

(Sentences have been aggregated to 3-8 Yrs.)

Interviewed: 1976   **Birthdate:** 1952   **Race:** White

36

had planned to escape from the institution by using the supervisor as a hostage. This inmate pulled a knife from his pocket, held it to the supervisor's throat and told him to lie on the bed. Almost simultaneously his accomplice struck the victim on the head with a soap sock and with his fists. This inmate attempted to stab the victim but the knife broke causing little damage from the stabbing. With the noise and confusion coming from the room, another boy notified his supervisor and both proceeded to the room. The other boy attempted to go to the aid of the supervisor but was told to stay back as this inmate held a knife to the throat of the victim. This inmate and his accomplice surrendered when numerous correctional officials appeared on the scene.

This inmate was released from Mid-State Penitentiary in October of 1971. He was arrested for burglary on two occasions within nine months after his release. He was arrested for the present offense less than two months after his release in 1971.

When questioned regarding his use of alcohol, he stated, "Too much, I don't drink all that often but when I do drink, I drink too much." When questioned regarding illegal drug usage, he stated, "Mostly yellow jackets or red devils, downers." He also stated that he has injected "yellow jackets" and "red devils." He further commented, "I never had a habit. I never stayed out long enough to get one. I didn't want one anyway — I couldn't afford it."

Additional Social History: During the interview, this inmate described himself as, "Just somebody that tried to stay out of the joint."

This inmate does not report receiving any vocational training prior to incarceration. He explains that since incarcerated, he has worked as a turbine operator for approximately 2-½ years from 1973 to 1975. He states that he received a vocational certificate in 1975 for on-the-job training as a turbine operator. He has expressed an interest in heavy equipment operation.

According to this inmate, he completed four years of school prior to incarceration. He reports receiving an 8th grade diploma in 1965 and a GED in 1970. He says he started two

37

Most Recently Admitted to the Correctional Environment: 1973

Criminal History: This inmate plead guilty to the offenses for which he is presently incarcerated. His records reveal that he burglarized a medical doctor's office. Acquisition of drugs appeared to be the reason for the break in.

This inmate's first recorded arrest was in April of 1967, for "curfew violation and investigation," and continued as follows: April of 1967, "struck father with a sledge hammer;" November of 1967, "runaway complaint;" March of 1968, "runaway;" April of 1968, "runaway complaint;" May of 1968, "runaway complaint." He was sentenced to a juvenile correctional facility in July of 1968 for burglary. In 1971, he was sentenced to a state penitentiary to serve 1-5 years for burglary. He was paroled in February of 1973, and was on parole five months later, when he committed the burglary for which he is presently incarcerated.

When questioned regarding his use of alcohol prior to incarceration, he stated, "I do not drink at all, I never have." When questioned regarding his use of illegal drugs prior to incarceration, he stated, "I never used drugs in my life, nor do I smoke or gamble."

His records indicate that he attempted to escape from the county jail prior to being received by the Department of Corrections. He received a consecutive 1-2 year sentence for "escape from Mid-State Penitentiary" in January of 1975.

Additional Social History: During the interview, this inmate commented, "I view myself as being 23, divorced, with very few prospects for a decent life after I leave here." He also stated, "I seen just about all there is to be seen. I have had happen just about all that can happen." He also relates that he was raped while incarcerated in a Northern Maximum Security Prison in 1971.

He states that he was raped on August 3, 1971, by four black inmates. He reports that after his sentence was imposed, he was sent to a Northern Maximum Security Prison. Seven days after he arrived, he and three others were raped by other inmates. The next morning after he told the inmates that he was going to report the incident to authorities, he was pushed from the upper cell block tier, where he fell a distance of 44 feet. Both feet were fractured, as well as his back. He was hospitalized for three months and was then transferred to Mid-State Penitentiary.

He explains that prior to incarceration he worked for the Penn Central Railroad and for two different sporting goods factories. When questioned regarding vocational training received since incarcerated, he responded, "absolutely none." He reports that he has no particular vocational interests and that he has been on an "unassigned gallery" (a row of cells where those inmates without jobs are housed) so long that it does not matter anymore. His records indicate that he has been on an unassigned gallery since November of 1974, in that jobs are not available for all inmates.

According to this inmate, he completed eight years of school and a GED in 1970 prior to incarceration. He states that he is not interested in college vocational courses.

His mother is employed as a caseworker by the State Department of Public Aid. However, his parents were divorced in 1954. His father has not remarried. This inmate stated that his mother was of great help to him when he returned on parole. Interestingly, his mother has been married four times. This inmate reports that he has four half-sisters and two half-brothers.

He states that he was married in March of 1973, and divorced in April of 1976. He tells that one child resulted from the marriage and that the child presently resides with his ex-wife in-state. He reports that he and his ex-wife stopped corresponding approximately one month ago.

Case #413

Offense: **Sentence:**

Theft (less than $150 in value)   6 Mos.
Theft (less than $150 in value)   6 Mos.

39

Forgery	3-9 Yrs.

(The sentences listed above were ordered to run concurrent)

Escape	3-9 Yrs.
Aggravated Battery	3-9 Yrs.
Theft (over $150 in value)	3-9 Yrs.
Theft (over $150 in value)	3-9 Yrs.

(All four sentences were ordered to run concurrent, but consecutive to the three concurrent sentences listed above)

(All sentences have been aggregated to 6-18 Yrs.)

Interviewed: 1976　　　　**Birthdate:** 1951　　　　**Race:** White

Most Recently Admitted to the Correctional Environment: 1973

Criminal History: This inmate plead guilty to the offenses for which he is presently incarcerated. His records reveal the following: One day in February of 1973, this inmate committed the offense of theft under $150 by taking cash money from the cash register of a service station. His two brothers participated in the offense with him.

Five days prior to the offense described above, this inmate took a carburetor, battery, fuel pump, and a set of license plates from an automobile, said property having a total value of less than $150.

Also in the same month this inmate forged a name and cashed two checks in the amount of $45. There were two other checks purported to be forged by this inmate (in the same amount of $45) for which he was not charged.

In March of 1973 while incarcerated in the county jail, this inmate, his two brothers and another prisoner grabbed a Deputy Sheriff, placed him in a cell, took his keys, changed their clothes, and escaped from jail. At the time of the jail break, this inmate and his three companions took the car of the Deputy Sheriff and used it as their means of escape. They later damaged the car extensively. It was a 1970 Mustang, having a value of more than $150.

It is further reported that this inmate did fight and wrestle with the Deputy Sheriff, at the time this inmate and others grabbed him and placed him in the cell just prior to their escape. This inmate was charged with aggravated battery because of the status of the Deputy Sheriff, i.e., a police officer. The aggravated battery charge was not because of serious injury suffered by the Deputy Sheriff. This inmate was also charged with a second offense of theft over $150.00 after he wrecked the Deputy Sheriff's car and stole a second auto valued at over $150.00.

This inmate explains that he was incarcerated in out-of-state juvenile facilities at age 16 for burglary. He explains that he escaped at age 17, was arrested, and released approximately four months later. He states that he was arrested again at age 18 for 3rd degree burglary and malicious trespassing for which he received two, six month sentences and a fine of $650 and court costs. His records indicate that he received a 1-10 year sentence for forgery in an adjacent state in 1971 and he explains that he was paroled in March of 1972. He was arrested for the present offenses less than one year after he was paroled. He describes his use of alcohol as "social" and does not report illegal drug usage.

Additional Social History: When questioned regarding his health, he stated, "I wouldn't say good." He asserts that he has brain damage. His records indicate that he is 5 ft. 8 in. tall and weighs 140 lbs.

This inmate reports that he received experience in the area of carpentry and installation of house siding prior to incarceration. He states that he is primarily interested in carpentry and siding work.

According to this inmate he completed 9 years of school prior to incarceration. He says he is "not that good at reading and writing" because he has always been a slow learner. He asserts that he is interested in acquiring a GED but he is not presently involved in an educational program.

He does not report ever having been married, but states that he has fathered one child. He relates that the child presently resides with the mother in an adjacent state.

He states that he has tried to enroll in group counseling in

41

the past and that he would like to become involved in group counseling. He says he recently completed a two-week career counseling program.

When questioned regarding his release plans, this inmate explained that he plans to marry the mother of his child and "settle down this time."

====

Case #414

Offense: **Sentence:**

Murder   50-100 Yrs.
Attempted Armed Robbery   50-100 Yrs.
Armed Robbery   8-20 Yrs.

(All sentences ordered to run concurrent)

Interviewed: 1976   **Birthdate:** 1951   **Race:** Black

Most Recently Admitted to the Correctional Environment: 1971

Criminal History: In 1970, this inmate and two companions attempted an armed robbery at an Iron and Metal Company. During the attempt, this inmate entered the office of the company and shot the paymaster through the heart, killing him. He plead not guilty. However, a jury found him guilty of the offenses of murder and attempted armed robbery. In 1971 he received a sentence of not less than 50 nor more than 100 years for each offense.

This inmate plead guilty to the armed robbery of a service station which occurred in 1969. Interestingly, this inmate was a fugitive from the county in which he later plead guilty to Armed Robbery (where he was awaiting a probation hearing) when he committed the above mentioned Murder and Armed Robbery. His records indicate a history of using weapons and a repeated penchant for violence. It is the considered opinion of the State's Attorney and sentencing judge that this inmate is totally unfit for parole and would present a dangerous menace to society if allowed to go free under parole conditions.

This inmate was first arrested in January of 1963, at age 11, for burglary and theft. He was arrested in June of 1963 for breaking and entering; purse snatching in July of 1963; curfew violation in February of 1965; disorderly conduct in February of 1965; disorderly conduct in September of 1965; fighting in September of 1965; and fighting in October of 1965. He was sent to a juvenile correctional facility as being incorrigible in 1965; was paroled in September of 1966; and was returned as a parole violator in September of 1967 for acts of violence.

As a parole violator in September of 1967, this inmate was charged with unlawful use of weapons, resisting arrest, and battery. He was transferred from a state boys' camp to a juvenile detention school in September of 1967, "for resisting supervision and pressuring his peers in camp." However, he was again paroled in May of 1968. When questioned regarding his past usage of alcohol, he commented, "just a little malt liquor." He does not report using illegal drugs other than marijuana.

Additional Social History: When questioned regarding his health, this inmate stated, "Good except for I lost my left eye (at a Northern Penitentiary) fighting."

During the interview, he stated, "I get along with most people basically. I like a little group. I get along all right in the institution."

According to this inmate, he has always been a barber. He reports that he presently has an apprentice license and has eight months to go before receiving a registered barber's license. He says he is primarily interested in barbering.

He states that he completed 11 years of school prior to incarceration. Although he has never completed a GED, he says he plans to get a GED and attend college after acquiring a registered barber's license.

He explains that he has two brothers presently incarcerated at Mid-State Penitentiary. He states that he has never been married. He reports fathering one child in 1968, but asserts that the child is now dead. He says he corresponds regularly with his

43

mother, brothers, and sisters, who presently reside in-state. He reports that his father died in 1973.

Case #415

Offense: **Sentence:**

Rape   15-45 Yrs.

Interviewed: 1976   **Birthdate:** 1951   **Race:** Black

Most Recently Admitted to the Correctional Environment: 1970

Criminal History: This inmate plead not guilty to the offense for which he is presently incarcerated. He was convicted by a jury verdict. His records reveal the following: One day in August of 1968, at 7:45 p.m. this inmate, who had been released by a juvenile correctional facility on parole earlier that day, arrived at the home of his aunt. His aunt let him in and told him there was cold lemonade in the refrigerator if he wished to have some. This inmate walked to the kitchen followed by his aunt's three year old son. This was the last time the 3 year old was seen alive. This inmate returned and his aunt asked where her son was. This inmate told her he was in the kitchen. His aunt started to walk toward the kitchen when this inmate put a knife to her throat, forced her into the bedroom and forced his aunt to have intercourse with him. The victim (this inmate's aunt) was screaming for her 3 year old son and managed to break away. This inmate caught her and stabbed her several times in the hall, and stabbed her several more times as she staggered into the kitchen. Eventually the victim managed to open her back door and let her dog in. The dog chased this inmate from her residence. The victim then ran as best she could to her neighbor's house and collapsed on the door step. During the rape this inmate reportedly told his aunt that her son was in the pantry. In the pantry the victim's three year

44

old son was found with a large cloth pushed into his mouth, so far that when removed his tongue could not be seen. The three year old died of suffocation from the rag.

When this inmate was arrested, a knife with blood stains on it was recovered from his possession (the same blood type as the victim). This inmate had a locker key in his possession when arrested, and when the locker was opened it was found to contain the clothing he wore on the date of the assault, saturated with blood, the same type as the victim.

A jury found this inmate guilty of rape and aggravated battery and not guilty of murder. The state recommended a sentence of 100-500 years in the state penitentiary.

This inmate explains that he was first arrested at age 15 for aggravated battery, in that he hit a man in the head with a stick. He says he was first sent to a juvenile correctional facility at age 15.

When questioned regarding the rape of his aunt, this inmate stated, "Our conversation led to a fight and that was it. She claimed I raped her and jumped on her." He does not report using alcohol or illegal drugs.

Additional Social History: This inmate stated that in his neighborhood other parents would complain to his parents about his aggressiveness toward their sons. "I would go down to the police station and nothing would come of it," he commented. This inmate says his mother often struck him on the head without valid reason, favoring his younger sister. He stated that his father drank to excess but was not physically abusive.

Materials received from a Northern State Penitentiary in 1973 indicated that he was involved in a fight with another inmate because he and the other inmate were competing for the homosexual favors of a third inmate. He has a history of aggressive behavior while incarcerated. The psychiatric evaluation, written in 1975, indicates that this inmate shows no evidence of guilt or concern about his past deeds. The psychiatrist evaluated him as an extremely dangerous, potentially aggressive individual.

He does not report receiving vocational training prior to incarceration. During the interview, he stated, "I'm not interested in vocational training." However, he says that he enjoys reading and writing.

According to this inmate, he completed eight years of school prior to incarceration. He states that he is presently involved in the GED program.

He does not report having been married or fathering children. He reports that his mother and father live in-state and that they correspond with him occasionally.

He says he plans to attend school when released.

Case #416

Offense: **Sentence:**

Burglary 6½-19½ Yrs.
Escape 6½-19½ Yrs.
Rape 7-20 Yrs.

(All sentences ordered to run concurrent)

Interviewed: 1976 **Birthdate:** 1950 **Race:** White

Most Recently Admitted to the Correctional Environment: 1973

Criminal History: This inmate plead guilty to the offenses for which he is presently incarcerated. His records reveal the following regarding the offense of rape: one November day in 1972, the victim (a 28 year-old woman) returned from her place of employment at approximately 7:00 p.m. She parked her automobile at the rear of her home, and as she was leaving her automobile she was accosted by this inmate in the alley and at knifepoint he forced her down to the ground, ripped off her clothes and undergarments, and covered her face with his jacket. He then proceeded to have intercourse with the victim. When the girl's grandmother came out of the rear of the house, this inmate picked up the victim, carried her down the alley, and threw her to the ground. Then he attempted to have sexual intercourse with her a second time. However, prior to completing the act a vehicle turned down the alley and this inmate ran away leaving his jacket and a packet of cigarettes behind. When he was arrested in January of 1973, he was identified by the victim in a lineup. At that time this inmate admitted the attack although he denied making penetration.

His records relate the following description of his behavior which lead to the burglary conviction. One day in January of 1973 this inmate entered a house when all of the residents were asleep and he found his way to the bedroom of a young female child. When the young girl woke up, this inmate attempted to choke her, and her screams awakened her brothers who were in another part of the home. The brothers ran into the bedroom and began to grapple with this inmate but he managed to jump out an open window and flee. In his haste to leave he left his coat and a black wallet containing numerous papers and items of identification. When he was apprehended in January he appeared in a lineup and was identified by the brothers as the perpetrator of the offense. This inmate then gave a statement to the police admitting he had entered the residence for the purpose of stealing money.

One day in April of 1973, this inmate (at that time incarcerated in the county jail on felony charges of rape and burglary) was participating in the garbage detail, i.e., he and other trusties of the county jail were removing cans of garbage to the area at the rear of the jail for purposes of disposal. While the other trusties were dumping garbage this inmate broke away from the area and jumped through a plate glass window which was in a jail door and escaped out of the jail area into the street. Sheriff's deputies immediately gave chase and other agencies including city and state police were notified of the escape. Within a matter of minutes after the escape this inmate was apprehended by city police officers. He was found hiding under a porch.

This inmate readily admits to burglary and escape but insists that he is not guilty of rape. He says he possesses no knowledge about the offense of rape. He asserts that he plead guilty to all three charges because he was threatened with a 20-60 year sentence for burglary if he did not.

This inmate reports that he was first arrested at age five or six for breaking into "the top part of a tavern" along with other children. He states that he was arrested approximately 10 times as a juvenile primarily for burglary and "a couple" auto thefts. He relates that he was sent to a juvenile correctional facility at age 16 for committing numerous burglaries. He says he was released at age 17 on juvenile parole and that he was arrested three days later for burglary. He received a prison sentence of 2-6 years for burglary in 1968 at age 17. He was paroled in November of 1971, and was not arrested again until January of 1973 (14 months later).

Additional Social History: He explains that he was born and reared in-state when he "wasn't locked up some place." He tells that he has three full brothers, three full sisters, one half-sister, and eight step-siblings. He states that he is the third oldest male and older than any of his full siblings. During our discussion, he commented that his mother had been married approximately seven different times to his real father and that she married his step-father in approximately 1964, and they presently reside in-state. He says he does not know where his "real father" presently resides. He relates that he was married in September of 1973 and divorced in 1974. He says one child resulted from the marriage and tells that his wife gave birth to a child out of wedlock prior to their marriage. He asserts that he "claims" both children.

This inmate states that he only completed seven years of school because he was "kicked out" in the 8th grade for fighting with a teacher. However, he reports receiving a GED at Mid-State in 1974 and asserts that he has accumulated approximately 50 semester hours toward an Associate of Arts degree in drafting technology.

According to this inmate, he acquired experience as a sheetmetal worker prior to incarceration. He tells that his father has been a sheetmetal worker for 25 or 30 years and that his father owns his own shop. He says he has received experience in welding, sheetmetal work, and drafting since incarcerated. He relates that he is primarily interested in drafting. His records indicate that the last time he was paroled he worked with his father on a sheetmetal job for approximately five months. Then he obtained piece work with a drywall company and worked there for five months, earning approximately $80 a week. He lost that job after he was placed in jail for being drunk and disorderly. After his release from the county jail, he couldn't find work for a month and then obtained employment with a laundry company where he worked in the washroom. He earned $2.55 an hour. In September of 1972, he married his wife who was 18 at the time with a 10 month old child.

This inmate describes his use of alcohol as "moderate" and does not report illegal drug usage other than marijuana.

During the interview, this inmate described himself as "moody." When questioned about his criminal history, he commented, "Most of it just running with different groups and messing around."

This inmate does not report having specific enemies at this or any other correctional facility. He further indicates that he is not having unusual difficulties adjusting to the correctional environment at the present time. However, he explains that he was beaten by approximately 20 black inmates at a Northern penitentiary in 1971. He says he fought a great deal at the Northern facility stating, "When a white enters (a Northern Penitentiary), he has three choices — fight, fuck, or break out."

During our discussion, he explained that his father had served approximately four years in a penitentiary for burglary in the 1940's. He asserts that his father beat him very severely when he caught him stealing, but that the beatings administered by his father were ineffective, in that he (this inmate) continued to steal. He states that at age 15, he was shot in the eye with a B.B. gun by his younger brother. Records indicate that he does not have control over his right eye and that it slants to the right. He says he plans to rejoin his wife and pursue drafting or sheetmetal work as an occupation when released from the penitentiary.

Case #417

Offense: **Sentence:**

Burglary   1-3 Yrs.

Burglary   2-6 Yrs.
Burglary   2-6 Yrs.

**(Both sentences ordered to run concurrent with each other,
but consecutive to the sentence of 1-3 listed above)**

Escape   1 Yr.-1 Yr. & 1 Day
(Ordered to run consecutive to the above sentences)
(All sentences aggregated to 4-10 Yrs. & 1 Day)

Interviewed: 1976,   **Birthdate:** 1950   **Race:** White

Most Recently Admitted to the Correctional Environment: 1972

Criminal History: This inmate plead guilty to the offenses for
which he is presently incarcerated. In January of 1972, he received
a sentence of 1-3 years for burglary. His records reveal the
following: One day in July of 1971, this inmate committed the
offense of burglary in that he did, without authority, knowingly
enter into a private residence with the intent to commit therein a
theft.

This inmate received parole in September of 1972 after
serving approximately nine months in prison for the offense of
burglary. He was arrested less than six months later for committing two additional burglaries and parole violation. In March
of 1973, he received two 2-6 year sentences for burglary. The
additional sentences were to run concurrent with each other but
consecutive to the initial sentence of 1-3 received in 1972 for
burglary. His records describe the two burglaries he plead guilty
to in 1973 as follows: The first burglary charge asserts that he
burglarized a church. The second burglary charge reports that he
burglarized a junior high school.

In May of 1975, this inmate escaped from Mid-State

Penitentiary. He was apprehended the following day and in July of 1975, received a consecutive sentence of 1 year to 1 year and 1 day for escape. All of the above mentioned sentences have been aggregated to a total of 4 years to 10 years and 1 day.

He received a sentence of six months in 1971 for aggravated battery. This inmate commented that the charge resulted from a family argument in which police officers became involved and a series of circumstances led to his stabbing a police officer.

According to this inmate, he was sent to juvenile correctional facilities at age 13 for running away from home. He says he was not released until October of 1968, at age 18. His records report that he was received at a juvenile facility in 1965 for committing the offense of theft and was discharged in 1966. His records further report that he was received at a second juvenile correctional facility in 1968 for committing the offense of theft and was discharged the same year. He describes his use of alcohol as "social." When questioned regarding illegal drug usage, he stated, "No, I've seen too many of my friends get wasted."

Additional Social History: During the interview, this inmate described himself as "just an everyday person." He further stated, "When I was young I never could converse with my parents. I was the type kid who wanted to be free to do what I wanted."

He explains that he was involved in a fight with a "chief" in the "Vice Lords" at a Northern State Penitentiary in 1973. However, he does not report having specific enemies at this or any other correctional facility in the state. He further indicates that he is not having unusual difficulties in adjusting to the correctional environment at the present time. His records indicate that he has received eight disciplinary tickets in the past five months for disregarding and disobeying orders and rules.

He explains that he received experience in auto body repair at an adult training center in 1970. Since incarcerated, he reports receiving a certificate for 9,000 hours in baking in 1974. He also reports receiving experience in house construction, i.e., roofing and remodeling.

According to this inmate, he completed nine years of school prior to incarceration. He states that he was in the education program at Mid-State Penitentiary in 1974 and 1975 but discontinued school in 1975 when assigned to the farm. He asserts

51

that educational facilities are not available on the farm. He says he is not presently interested in acquiring a GED because, "a lot of guys in the school right now — all they want to do is play."

He relates that he was married in 1973 and that he and his wife separated approximately one day later. He says they are presently getting a divorce. He indicates that he corresponds intermittently with his mother and father who reside in-state.

Case #417

Offense: **Sentence:**

Burglary   1-3 YRS

Burglary   2-6 YRS
Burglary   2-6 YRS

(Both sentences ordered to run concurrent with each other, but consecutive to the sentence of 1-3 listed above)

Escape   1 YR-1 YR & 1 Day
(Ordered to run consecutive to the above sentences)
(All sentences Aggregated to 4-10 YRS & 1 Day)

Interviewed: 1976,   **Birthdate:** 1950   **Race:** White

Most Recently Admitted to the Correctional Environment: 1973

Criminal History: This inmate plead guilty to the offenses for which he is presently incarcerated. In January of 1972, he received a sentence of 1-3 years for burglary. His records reveal the following: One day in July of 1971, this inmate committed the offense of burglary in that he did, without authority, knowingly enter into a private residence with the intent to commit therein a theft.

This inmate received parole in September of 1972 after

serving approximately nine months in prison for the offense of burglary. He was arrested less than six months later for committing two additional burglaries and parole violation. In March of 1973, he received two 2-6 year sentences for burglary. The additional sentences were to run concurrent with each other but consecutive to the initial sentence of 1-3 received in 1972 for burglary. His records describe the two burglaries he plead guilty to in 1973 as follows: The first burglary charge asserts that he burglarized a church. The second burglary charge reports that he burglarized a junior high school.

In May of 1975, this inmate escaped from Mid-State Penitentiary. He was apprehended the following day and in July of 1975, received a consecutive sentence of 1 year to 1 year and 1 day for escape. All of the above mentioned sentences have been aggregated to a total of 4 years to 10 years and 1 day.

He received a sentence of six months in 1971 for aggravated battery. This inmate commented that the charge resulted from a family argument in which police officers became involved and a series of circumstances led to his stabbing a police officer.

According to this inmate, he was sent to juvenile correctional facilities at age 13 for running away from home. He says he was not released until October of 1968, at age 18. His records report that he was received at a juvenile facility in 1965 for committing the offense of theft and was discharged in 1966. His records further report that he was received at a second juvenile correctional facility in 1968 for committing the offense of theft and was discharged the same year. He describes his use of alcohol as "social." When questioned regarding illegal drug usage, he stated, "No, I've seen too many of my friends get wasted."

Additional Social History: During the interview, this inmate described himself as "just an everyday person." He further stated, "When I was young I never could converse with my parents. I was the type kid who wanted to be free to do what I wanted."

He explains that he was involved in a fight with a "chief" in the "Vice Lords" at a Northern State Penitentiary in 1973. However, he does not report having specific enemies at this or any other correctional facility in the state. He further indicates that he is not having unusual difficulties in adjusting to the correctional environment at the present time. His records indicate that he has received eight disciplinary tickets in the past five months for disregarding and disobeying orders and rules.

He explains that he received experience in auto body repair at an adult training center in 1970. Since incarcerated, he reports receiving a certificate for 9,000 hours in baking in 1974. He also reports receiving experience in house construction, i.e., roofing and remodeling.

According to this inmate, he completed nine years of school prior to incarceration. He states that he was in the education program at Mid-State Penitentiary in 1974 and 1975 but discontinued school in 1975 when assigned to the farm. He asserts that educational facilities are not available on the farm. He says he is not presently interested in acquiring a GED because, "a lot of guys in the school right now — all they want to do is play."

He relates that he was married in 1973 and that he and his wife separated approximately one day later. He says they are presently getting a divorce. He indicates that he corresponds intermittently with his mother and father who reside in-state.

He tells that he was involved in group counseling for approximately three months in 1975. When questioned regarding release plans, he stated, "Go out there and try and stay straight."

Case #418

Offense:	**Sentence:**
Armed Robbery	5-15 YRS
Armed Robbery	7-21 YRS
Armed Robbery	20-40 YRS
Armed Robbery	20-40 YRS

Armed Robbery	20-40 YRS
Armed Robbery	20-40 YRS
Armed Robbery	20-40 YRS
Armed Robbery	20-40 YRS

(All sentences ordered to run concurrent)

Interviewed: 1976   **Birthdate:** 1950   **Race:** White

Most Recently Admitted to the Correctional Environment: 1972

Criminal History: This inmate plead guilty to seven counts of Armed Robbery and not guilty to one count of Armed Robbery. His records reveal the following: One day in March of 1971, at approximately 9:15 a.m., this inmate entered a food store. He took an item to the counter and then pulled out a shotgun and ordered the clerk to empty the cash register and give him all the money. He then asked one of the customers in the store for the money from his wallet. This inmate then ordered all the customers into a backroom and left the store. The total amount taken from all sources was approximately $330.00.

Five days later, at approximately 10:45 a.m., this inmate entered another food store, pulled out a handgun, and ordered the clerk to give him all the money from the register. After this was accomplished, this inmate left the store. The total amount taken from the store was approximately $150.00.

The next day at approximately 8:30 p.m., this inmate and an accomplice entered a tavern. They ordered a beer and shortly afterwards announced to the owner that it was a holdup. This inmate pulled out a handgun and ordered the owner to give him all the money from the cash register (approximately $60.00). The two men then took the wallet of a customer and a small amount of change that was on top of the bar and left the establishment.

Two days later, at approximately 9:15 a.m., this inmate entered a food market. He walked to the counter carrying a small pie; pulled out a handgun and ordered the clerk to put all the money from the register into a paper bag. He then asked the owner and a bread truck driver for their wallets and left the store. The total amount taken from all sources was approximately $150.00.

Two weeks later, at approximately 10:00 p.m., this inmate and an accomplice entered a liquor store. This inmate walked to the counter carrying a bottle of whiskey, opened up his jacket, and showed the clerk a sawed-off shotgun. This inmate then ordered the clerk to place all the money from the register into a bag (approximately $600.00). This inmate and his accomplice ordered both clerks to lie down behind the counter and then left the store.

One day in August of 1971, at approximately 12:30 p.m., this inmate and an accomplice entered a tavern. This inmate ordered a few drinks from the bartender, and after approximately one-half hour, this inmate pulled out a shotgun and ordered the bartender to place all the money from the register into a paper bag. This inmate then ordered two customers to place their money into the same bag. The total amount taken from the tavern was approximately $500.00.

Eight days later at approximately 8:15 a.m., this inmate and an accomplice entered a tavern and ordered drinks from the bartender. A man entered the tavern to cash a check, and while the transaction was in process this inmate pulled out a sawed-off shotgun and ordered the bartender to give him all the money from the safe. The bartender complied with his order and placed approximately $2,000.00 into a cloth bag. After this was accomplished, this inmate and his accomplice left the establishment.

Seven days later, at approximately 2:30 p.m., this inmate and an accomplice entered a liquor store. This inmate showed the clerk a small handgun and ordered him to place all the money from the register into a brown bag. Taken from the register was approximately $525.00. This inmate and his accomplice then left the store and entered an automobile. Pursuant to a radio message, the car was stopped approximately twenty minutes later by city police. At that time his accomplice was arrested but this inmate fled from the arresting officer. A warrant was issued for his arrest and he was subsequently arrested by county police in California, in September of 1971.

One evening in April of 1972, this inmate and three other inmates were involved in an alleged attempted escape. One of the inmates grabbed a jailer and removed the keys to the cellblock, and this inmate punched the jailer in the face. Subsequently, a trusty helped foil the escape attempt.

The state's attorney's office, as part of the agreement for this inmate's guilty plea, agreed that they would not prosecute for the offenses of attempted escape and aggravated battery.

This inmate explains that he was first incarcerated as a juvenile at age sixteen for burglary. He received a one to three year sentence for burglary in October of 1968, and was paroled in July of 1970. Thus, this inmate committed eight armed robberies in less than thirteen months after receiving parole for the offense of burglary.

He describes his use of alcohol as "very little" and does not report illegal drug usage.

Additional Social History: During the interview, this inmate stated, "It seems to me I've always been a petty little thief since I was a youngster." He further commented that if his parents didn't give him money and he could not earn it, he would steal it.

He explains that prior to incarceration, he received experience as a welder, burner, and crane operator. Since incarcerated, he says he has received landscaping experience. He states that he is interested in "hospital work." However, he indicates that he is primarily interested in living as a nomad, "traveling around" and working when necessary.

According to this inmate, he completed nine years of school prior to incarceration. He relates that he received a GED in 1972 or 1973 at Mid-State Penitentiary. He tells that he has presently completed approximately twenty semester hours of college. He comments that he is primarily interested in English, speech, and dramatics.

He does not report marrying or fathering children. He states that his parents presently reside in-state. He says his parents visit him when he requests a visit and he calls them regularly.

When questioned regarding his release plans, he explained that he plans to reside with his parents. As mentioned earlier, he intends to "travel around," living as a nomad, working only when necessary.

Case #419

Offense: **Sentence:**

Murder   18-40 YRS

Interviewed: 1976   **Birthdate:** 1950   **Race:** White

Most Recently Admitted to the Correctional Environment: 1972

Criminal History: This inmate plead not guilty to the offense for which he is presently incarcerated. He was convicted by a jury verdict of burglarizing a private residence and killing a woman by striking her with a piece of wood during the burglary. His records reveal that he has committed offenses related to disorderly types of conduct, traffic offenses, firearms violations, attempted armed robbery, and reckless conduct. He reports that in 1969, after having been discharged from a juvenile correctional facility, he was sentenced to serve one year at a state farm for "reckless conduct." He explains that the initial charge was armed robbery but that it was reduced to "reckless conduct." He describes his use of alcohol as "very light" and does not report illegal drug usage other than marijuana.

Additional Social History: During our discussion, this inmate indicated that the difficulties he had as a juvenile were "just for the hell of it."

He explains that he worked as a truck driver and machine operator prior to incarceration. Since incarcerated, he says he has received approximately two years of training working in the prison hospital. He does not report receiving vocational certificates in any field. He states that he is presently a knitter at the Knit Shop. He asserts that he is primarily interested in becoming a paramedic.

According to this inmate, he quit school during his 10th year, but received a GED in 1967. He explains that he took a college course in 1975 but did not complete it. He says he would like to enroll in a paramedic program.

58

He reports that he was married in 1971 and divorced in 1974. He does not report ever fathering children. He tells that he corresponds with his mother and father in-state.

Case #420

Offense: **Sentence**

Rape   4-12 YRS
Robbery   4-12 YRS

(All sentences ordered to run concurrent)

Interviewed: 1976   **Birthdate:** 1950   **Race:** White

Most Recently Admitted to the Correctional Environment: 1972

Criminal History: A psychiatric evaluation written in February of 1975, classified this inmate as follows: He is not psychotic and he has no symptoms of neurosis. From the psychiatric point of view, he has a personality disorder of the anti-social type. That means that the hopes of him changing his lifestyle are very little.

    This inmate plead not guilty to the offenses for which he is presently incarcerated. He was convicted by a bench verdict. His records reveal the following: One day in July of 1972, at 9:30 a.m. on an urban avenue, the victims were approached from behind by this inmate. He forced them into an area next to the railroad tracks. He then proceeded to alternately rape the victims and then fled. The victims then called the police and gave a description of their attacker. The inmate was arrested "minutes later", approximately three blocks from the scene of the attack. This inmate was initially indicted for committing two offenses of "deviate sexual assault" in that he forced the victims, two young women under the age of 18 years, to alternately perform an act of oral copulation upon him; two offenses of "contributing to the sexual delinquency of a child", in that he performed acts of intercourse with the two female children (under the age of 18 years); two offenses of "rape"; and two offenses of "robbery." This inmate explains the circumstances which led to his present incarceration as a situation in which a 16 or 17 year old female acquaintance was attempting to "rip him off" for approximately $1800 involved in the sale of narcotics.

His records relate the following regarding his juvenile record: He has a long history of early delinquency, including eleven station adjustments and four complaints. The station adjustments include: arson, damage to property and incorrigibility, truancy, theft from his father, glue sniffing, possession of fireworks, runaway, and poor adjustment in school. This inmate has also been charged with petty theft and theft from a mail box. Subsequently, in August of 1965, he was placed in a juvenile correctional facility by the county court for his involvement in the burglary of a neighbor's apartment.

This inmate states that he was paroled from a juvenile facility in February of 1966, but subsequently returned as a parole violator and was later transferred to a second juvenile facility because of an escape attempt at the first. He was reparoled in 1967, and during the four months he was on parole, he was returned to the juvenile reception center on two occasions; the first time as a returned parolee in April, 1967. However, he was allowed to resume parole in May, but was returned as a "guest" in June, 1967, and his guest status was dropped three days later. During the time of his last juvenile parole, he ran away to California, was involved in sexual delinquency with a 13 year old girl, and was apprehended by police on suspicion of burglary and curfew violation. He was released and was later apprehended in June of 1967, for his involvement in an armed robbery. The armed robbery apparently stemmed from an earlier burglary in June of 1967, when numerous guns and ammunition were stolen.

In September of 1967, he received a 1-5 year sentence for aggravated battery. His records relate the following description of the offense: One evening, at approximately 7:45 p.m., a supervisor at the Morris Industrial School for Boys was attacked by this inmate and an accomplice (also a juvenile inmate). This inmate and his accomplice were roommates and

60

SEE PAGE 37

college courses in 1973 but did not complete either of them. During the interview, he commented, "I don't write too good but I read good." He impressed this interviewer as needing additional education, but not at the college level. His speech appears inconsistent with his recorded educational achievement and this inmate seems to be cognizant of a serious writing deficiency.

He does not report ever having been married. When asked if he had ever fathered a child, he stated, "I'm supposed to have one, but I've never seen it." He explains that "his child lives with the mother."

When questioned regarding his release plans, this inmate asserted that he planned to "get the hell out of (the state in which Mid-State Penitentiary is located)."

Case #421

Offense: **Sentence:**

Rape & Indecent Liberties with child   7-11 Yrs.
Aggravated Battery   3-9 Yrs.

(Sentences have been aggregated to 10-20 years)

Interviewed: 1976   **Birthdate:** 1949   **Race:** Black

Most Recently Admitted to the Correctional Environment: 1969

Criminal History: In 1969, this inmate received a sentence of 7-11 years for rape and indecent liberties with a child. In 1972, he received a consecutive sentence of 3-9 years for aggravated battery. Since that time, his sentences have been aggregated to a total of 10-20 years.

One day in March of 1969 at approximately 4:00 p.m. this inmate raped a twelve year old girl. This inmate lured the victim into his house one cold afternoon while the girl was waiting for her parents in front of his house. She entered through the front door and this inmate told her to go into the kitchen in the rear of the house. She refused and he grabbed her by the arm and forced her into the kitchen. One of the burners on the stove was lit and she warmed her hands for a couple of minutes over the burner. This inmate then told the girl that he wanted her to "give him some." She said she would not do this because her mother had told her not to do that and she did not want to do it anyway. This inmate then picked up a saw which had been lying on the sink in the kitchen, and brandishing it in front of her, told her that if she did not do what he wanted her to do he would cut her head off with the saw. He then threw her on a cot located in the kitchen and proceeded to pull her skirt up and her panties down. She reportedly continued to resist, at which time he again threatened her with the saw. He then climbed on top of her and had intercourse with her. After the act was completed the victim put her panties back on and ran out of the house.

After telling the story to the police, the victim was taken to the emergency room at a local hospital, where she was examined by a doctor. The doctor testified that the child's hymen was ruptured, that there was a considerable amount of blood in her vagina, and that there was presence of sperm in her vagina. The presence of sperm was corroborated by a second doctor who ran microscopic tests. Several items of the victim's clothing were sent to the State Crime Laboratory and a crime analyst testified as to the presence of seminal stains on the victim's panties, skirt, and half slip.

This inmate plead not guilty to the offenses of rape and indecent liberties with a child and was convicted by a jury verdict.

This inmate plead guilty to the offense of aggravated battery in that he assaulted a prison guard while incarcerated in a state penitentiary serving his previously received sentence of 7-11 years for the offense of rape.

His records reveal the following description of the offense: one day in January of 1972, at approximately 2:00 p.m., this inmate left his cell without authorization. The tower guard ordered this inmate to go back into his cell. This inmate refused. After several warnings the tower guard made a phone

62

call and asked the Lieutenant to come to the cellhouse. The tower guard then asked this inmate his name and number. A few minutes later the Lieutenant arrived at the cellhouse and asked this inmate to follow him to detention. This inmate refused. Thus, the Lieutenant ordered this inmate back to his cell. The Lieutenant then left the area.

After the Lieutenant left the area, the tower guard sat down at the cellhouse keeper's desk where he proceeded to write the report in the log book. As he was so occupied, he heard someone shouting "I'm going to kill him." The tower guard looked up and saw this inmate coming toward him with two pieces of pipe. The tower guard got up from his desk and picked up his chair in an attempt to prevent being hit by this inmate. This inmate chased the guard around the desk, swinging the pipes at all times. After one complete revolution around the desk, this inmate struck the tower guard in the side of the head. The tower guard then dropped the chair, and fell across the floor toward the entrance hall of the cellhouse, with this inmate in pursuit. The tower guard then attempted to go up the steps leading to the cellhouse door but was struck again and fell to the floor. At this point, several inmates intervened and disarmed this inmate. As a result of the attack, the tower guard suffered a severe head wound which required seven stitches. The tower guard had to undergo two surgical operations which required extensive physical therapy. Physicians' reports indicate that the tower guard suffered permanent disability.

Regarding the offenses of rape and indecent liberties with a child, this inmate asserts that he had nothing to do with the offenses and claims he was framed. When questioned about the aggravated battery conviction, this inmate claimed he was fighting three inmates and a guard "got in the way." He further commented that he was not sure if he hit the guard or not because he was fighting three inmates that jumped him.

This inmate reports that he was first arrested at age 13 for auto theft. He relates that he was sent to a juvenile correctional facility in Mississippi where he remained for one year and one month. His records indicate that he was arrested for auto larceny, declared incorrigible and remanded to criminal court for trial in February of 1967. His records also indicate an arrest for curfew violation in May of 1968 and an arrest for being in possession of fictitious plates and not having a driver's license in October of 1968.

Additional Social History: This inmate was born in Tennessee. He attended a school in Mississippi from the first to the tenth grade. This inmate tells that he and a woman lived in a common-law relationship from 1967 to 1969. He does not report fathering children. He explains that his mother presently resides out of state, and that his father resides in-state. He further commented that he corresponds with his mother on a regular basis but does not write to or receive letters from his father.

According to this inmate he completed nine years of school prior to incarceration. He asserts that he acquired a GED in February or March of this year and expressed an interest in college.

He reports receiving "a little" auto mechanics experience prior to incarceration. When questioned regarding vocational training received since incarcerated, he stated, "Mostly everything in the entertainment field." This inmate claims to have written, "Twelve manuscripts, six scripts for movies, and things." He further commented, "I just created a new magazine called the 'All Seeing Eye'." He asserts "that page would be covered if you were to write about all my talents and skills." Psychiatric and psychological evaluations included in this inmate's master record file indicate that he is of low average intelligence.

This inmate's behavioral history is one of violence since incarcerated. At a Northern prison from September of 1969 to June of 1971 this inmate received a total of 36 disciplinary reports, 11 of which resulted in segregation placement. His most serious rule violations as of June, 1971 consisted of fighting with inmates.

This inmate was transferred from one maximum security prison to a second Northern maximum security prison by the Reception and Diagnostic Team at the first prison. At that time the diagnostic team's impression was that this inmate "will not cause any trouble in the inmate population between himself and officers (guards) but that his difficulty lies in getting along with other inmates."

It should, of course, be remembered that seven months after this inmate's transfer to the second Northern maximum security prison he committed the offense of aggravated battery upon a guard. Eight months later in August of 1972, this inmate caused such a disturbance in the detention hospital of the prison that the guard in charge filed an incident report. The following day a different guard filed an incident report because this inmate refused to return to his cell as he had on the previous day. This inmate was eventually returned to the Reception and Classification Unit at the first maximum security prison he was assigned to and in February of 1974 hc was transferred to Mid-State penitentiary.

Prior to his arrival at Mid-State penitentiary he had received five disciplinary reports for fighting and numerous others for offenses such as "being in wrong cell," "not obeying a direct order and lying to cell Sergeant," "being out of his cell without permission," "refusing an assignment and destroying state property," "having contraband in cell," "being off his assignment," etc. After serving 28 months at Mid-State, he has received 28 disciplinary tickets. He has received disciplinary reports for such offenses as disobeying orders, causing a disturbance, improper conduct, unauthorized movement, possessing contraband, and fighting on three occasions. This inmate received a disciplinary ticket for "assault on or fighting with employee or resident" as recent as May of 1976. In a conversation with a correctional officer at Mid-State, it was reported to me that this inmate is a prominent "gang leader." He denies using alcohol and/or illegal drugs.

During our discussion this inmate asserted that he had been involved in approximately 25 fights with other inmates. He says over the past years of his incarceration he has been in numerous fights with "Lords," "Stones," and "D's." He describes himself stating, "outspoken, very aggressive, versatile, I'm some of everything." In addition he commented, "Since I've been locked up I've gone into cartooning, I've recorded a record, and does magazine designs." This inmate claims to be so talented and skilled that it would take a considerable amount of paper to list said talents and skills.

He was placed in Segregation in March of 1976, for investigation concerning his involvement in the sexual attack of another inmate. The inmate attacked was a young Caucasian who reportedly "did not tell anyone he was assaulted until three days later when he slashed his wrists in a suicide attempt." Materials in this inmate's master record file indicate that while incarcerated he has been involved in sexual activity with young Caucasian inmates. Most recently he received a disciplinary ticket in May of this year for fighting. During the hearing he reportedly stated that the inmate he was allegedly fighting "has been having troubles on 8 Gallery. I just put my hand on his head. The Officer was only three feet away. I paid the Vice Lords $15 to stop messing with him."

If one was to rely on this inmate's reported strengths and accomplishments, the length of the list would be staggering. However, he apparently has a propensity to report fiction as truth as well as blatant prevarication when he feels it is to his advantage. For example, this examiner called the education department to verify his acquisition of a GED at Mid-State in February or March of this year as he claims. I was informed that this inmate does not have a GED and did not take the exam as he stated during the interview. Thus, the only strength this writer has detected after interviewing this inmate and reading his master record file is his apparent physical strength and his ability to report false information in a forthright and unflinching manner.

When asked if he was interested in group counseling, he asserted that he has his own "group therapy" and does it to himself.

Case #422

Offense:

Rape
Aggravated Battery
Murder

Sentence:

20-40 Yrs.
5-10 Yrs.
100-300 Yrs.

Interviewed: 1976   **Birthdate:** 1949   **Race:** Black

Most Recently Admitted to the Correctional Environment: 1972

Criminal History: This inmate plead not guilty to the offenses for which he is presently incarcerated. He was convicted of rape and aggravated battery by a jury verdict and received a sentence of twenty to forty years and five to ten years in May of 1972. His records reveal the following: This inmate accosted the victim in her basement as she laundered her clothes, at which time he forced her to have sexual intercourse with him, compelled her to submit to an act of oral copulation and then proceeded to beat her into bloody unconsciousness with a baseball bat. Before beating her, he told her he had to do something with her to keep her from identifying him. She remained hospitalized for seven days, sustaining a broken finger, a broken jaw, and also slight burns about the body where he attempted to force her into a burning boiler type furnace.

This inmate was convicted of murder by a jury verdict and received a sentence of one hundred to three hundred years in August of 1973, (the state's recommendation was two hundred to six hundred years). His records reveal the following : One day in October of 1970, at 11:45 p.m., this inmate forced open a living room window in the home of the victim and entered the darkened home. This inmate then proceeded to the kitchen where he found a carving knife that was twelve and one-half inches in length. Then, while armed with this knife, he crept upstairs to the bedrooms of the house. Asleep in the house at the time was the victim, her daughter, and her three year old son. Once upstairs, this inmate attacked the victim as she lay asleep in her bedroom dressed only in a nightgown. At knifepoint, this inmate raped her and when finished, plunged the twelve-inch carving knife into her heart and again into her side, killing her. This inmate then stole two purses and fled.

This inmate then went through the backyards of two of the victim's neighbors and then into the garage of one of the neighbors, where he ransacked the two purses (leaving his thumbprint on one of the articles in the purse).

In July of 1973, this inmate received a sentence of two years to two years and one day (to run concurrent with sentences of twenty to forty years and five to ten years for rape and aggravated battery) after pleading guilty to the charge of robbery. The robbery sentence has now been served.

During the interview, this inmate explained that he grew up in juvenile correctional facilities. He says he was first sentenced as a juvenile at age twelve for truancy, returned to juvenile facilities at age thirteen for rape, and was then returned intermittently for violations of juvenile parole until finally released at age seventeen. Records received from the Middletown Police Department indicate that he was arrested in April of 1970, for contributing to the sexual delinquency of a child; in June of 1970 for being disorderly and mob action; July of 1970 for theft; November of 1970 for rape; theft in January of 1971 (received three years probation — first thirty days to be served in jail and $2,000.00 restitution). His records also indicate that he was arrested for grand theft in February of 1971 and arrested for grand theft, resisting police, and traffic violations in March of 1971. He describes his use of alcohol as "social-light" and does not report using illegal drugs.

Additional Social History: During our discussion, this inmate stated that he has been "tensed up" since being sent to prison. He asserts that he's an energetic person and stated, "Being an energetic person, I likes to move." He further stated, "I'm very changeable — I be telling somebody the truth and if they try to distort it, I get very upset." He argues that you have to be a "politician" or a "snitch" or "you don't have anything coming."

His records from a Northern State Penitentiary report that he attempted to hang himself in the isolation and segregation building in July of 1975. A Psychiatric Progress Report at that time stated, "No formal mental illness found. Antisocial personality with situational reaction of young adult life." This inmate's intellectual functioning has been evaluated as about "dull normal range." This inmate also has a history of "Black Peace-Stone" membership.

He does not report having enemies at this or any other

correctional facility in the state.

This inmate claims to have experience in masonry, shoe repair, electronics, and drill press operations. He states that he has not received any vocational training "to speak of" since incarcerated. He asserts, "It's hard to hold an interest in here because it's too hard to get a job."

According to this inmate, the majority of his education was received in juvenile correctional facilities. He relates that he received a GED at one such institution in 1965 or 1966.

He explains that although he has never been married, he has fathered one child, but he does not know where the child or mother resides. He states that his father died in 1965 or 1966. He says he corresponds with his mother, aunts, cousins, and sister who presently reside in-state.

=====

Case #423

Offense: **Sentence:**

Armed Robbery   4-8 Yrs.
Attempted Murder   5-10 Yrs.

(Sentences have been aggregated to 9-18 Yrs.)

Interviewed: 1976   **Birthdate:** 1948   **Race:** Black

Most Recently Admitted to the Correctional Environment: 1973

Criminal History: This inmate plead guilty to the offenses for which he is presently incarcerated. His records reveal that he was received at Mid-State Penitentiary in April of 1968, to serve a 5-10 year sentence for attempted murder in connection with the armed robbery of two women. He shot one of the women when, according to his records, he reached into the front seat and grabbed the women's purses but one of the victims held on to her purse and the gun which this inmate was holding discharged wounding the lady in the fleshy portion of her right

69

side. This inmate was paroled in October of 1972, and committed the offense of armed robbery in March of 1973, in that he and an accomplice entered a residential apartment and robbed a man and his girlfriend at gun point.

This inmate claims that he was first sent to a juvenile correctional facility at age 15 for operating a motor vehicle without a license. He says he served approximately seven months. He states that he was arrested approximately six times as a juvenile for offenses such as burglary, curfew violations, and running away from home. He comments that he first ran away from home when he was eight years old. He received a one year sentence for theft in 1966. He paid a fine for disorderly conduct in 1967. He describes his use of alcohol as "social" and does not report illegal drug usage other than marijuana.

Additional Social History: During the interview, this inmate stated, "On the streets, I don't have no trouble except money. I get along with everybody." During the interview, he was polite and cooperative.

He states that he did not possess any vocational skills prior to incarceration. Since incarcerated, he tells that he has acquired experience in slaughtering and meat processing, tailoring, and welding.

According to this inmate, he completed eight years of school prior to incarceration. He explains that although he was involved in the educational program at Mid-State Penitentiary in 1973 he did not acquire a GED. When asked why he quit the program, he stated, "I got tired of that East House."

His records relate the following about his family background: He is the product of a very unstable home environment. The family structure was broken by separation of the parents when this inmate was ten years old. Indications are that the parents continually argued and drank heavily when they were living together. It is reported that the subject's father was incarcerated in the Michigan State Penitentiary for allegedly killing another man. The mother was dependent on ADC payments she received in order to support her four children. An older sister, along with her three illegitimate children, resided with the mother. A younger brother has been

70

in the Middletown State Hospital and in the Centerville State School for what is believed to be permanent brain damage. At one point in this inmate's childhood he was declared a dependent minor and placed in a foster home for three years. He then returned to live with his mother where he remained until his incarceration in April, 1968. He does not report ever having been married. He states that he fathered a child (female) in 1968. He reports that the child lives with the mother in an adjacent state.

When questioned regarding his interest in group counseling, he stated, "Quit group counseling last year, got tired of going over there, they'd tell ya how to make plans for parole. It really wasn't nothing." He says he would like to be paroled and "get a job at Caterpillar."

Case #424

Offense: **Sentence:**

Arson   15-20 Yrs.
Arson   15-20 Yrs.
Murder   15-30 Yrs.

(All sentences ordered to run concurrent)

Interviewed: 1976   **Birthdate:** 1947   **Race:** White

Most Recently Admitted to the Correctional Environment: 1965

Criminal History: This inmate plead not guilty to the offenses for which he is presently incarcerated. His records reveal that he set fire to a hardware store at approximately 9 a.m. and a six story business building at approximately 11:30 a.m. on the same day in 1964. A fireman was killed when a section of one of the buildings collapsed while attempts were being made to quash the fire. His records also indicate that he started two fires in 1963, one of which resulted in two deaths.

His records further indicate that he was paroled from a juvenile correctional facility less than three weeks before committing the offenses for which he is presently incarcerated. He explains that he was incarcerated in approximately six different juvenile facilities for offenses such as robbery and burglary. He does not report using alcohol and/or illegal drugs.

Additional Social History: During the interview he stated, "I'm what you call a loser either way it goes." He explains that he has had a problem with his nerves since 1971, when his mother died. He indicates that he treats people the way he perceives they are treating him.

Throughout our discussion, he emphasized his educational accomplishments and is obviously very proud of said accomplishments. He reports completing eight years of school prior to incarceration. He tells that he has attended school at Mid-State for the past year. According to this inmate he recently passed the preliminary exam for the GED and will be taking the GED exam next month. He appears very interested in education at this point in time, takes a great deal of pride in his educational accomplishments, and plans to eventually study electronics. He explains that he is primarily interested in electronics.

He states that he has never married or fathered children. He relates that his mother and father are presently deceased. His father reportedly "drank himself to death." He explains that his father would frequently mistreat and physically assault his (this inmate's) mother.

He explains that he was involved in group counseling in the past, but it interfered with school so he discontinued the program.

He relates that he does not have specific release plans at this point in time, but asserts that he is interested in halfway house placement.

Case #425

Offense: **Sentence:**

Murder   30-60 Yrs.

Interviewed: 1976   **Birthdate:** 1947   **Race:** White

Most Recently Admitted to the Correctional Environment: 1965

Criminal History: This inmate along with three male associates, argued with and beat a young man with their fists and with a hedge post resulting in the victim's death. This inmate explains that he was sent to a juvenile correctional facility on three or four occasions for offenses related to alcohol. He states that prior to his incarceration, he consumed approximately a "fifth" of alcohol per day. He says he has never used illegal drugs.

Additional Social History: During the interview, he stated, "I ain't got a real low opinion of myself but then sometimes I do." He continued, "I try not to go down too far." He is candid in explaining that his past and present incarceration has been extremely frustrating and his desire for release is amply apparent.

He explains that he has experience as a butcher and as a machinist. He has expressed an interest in construction work and heavy equipment operation.

He states that he completed seven years of school prior to incarceration. He says he studied for the GED at a Northern penitentiary, but did not take the examinations. He has expressed an interest in acquiring a GED at Mid-State Penitentiary.

He explains that he has never married. He tells that he corresponds with his mother, sisters, and brothers on a regular basis. He says his father is deceased.

During our discussion, he informed this interviewer that he

plans to acquire a job in the area of construction and/or heavy equipment operation when released.

===

Case #426

Offense: **Sentence:**

Grand Theft   5-10 Yrs.
Aggravated Kidnapping   8-12 Yrs.
Aggravated Kidnapping   8-12 Yrs.
Rape   8-12 Yrs.

(All sentences ordered to run concurrent)

Interviewed: 1976   **Birthdate:** 1947   **Race:** White

Most Recently Admitted to the Correctional Environment: 1973

Criminal History: This inmate plead guilty to the offenses for which he is presently incarcerated. His records reveal the following: (Aggravated Kidnapping) One day in November of 1972, this inmate forced a woman into his auto. After beating her and threatening her with death he forced her to have intercourse with him. Afterwards he again threatened to kill her if she attempted to escape. The victim subsequently escaped and positively identified him in a line up.

(Aggravated Kidnapping) Two days later this inmate forced a 15 year old girl into his car while armed with a pair of scissors. After beating the victim he forced her to have intercourse with him under the threat of death. The victim required internal surgery and 35 stitches to repair the internal damage, in that some external object was forced into her vagina.

(Rape) One day in December of 1972, this inmate forced a 16 year old girl into his auto while armed with a pair of scissors. After beating her he forcibly removed her clothes and

74

forced her to have intercourse. The victim was beaten and threatened with death.

(Grand Theft) Twenty days later, this inmate stole an automobile from a large metropolitan airport. He was subsequently arrested in possession of the automobile.

During the interview, this inmate asserted that he had only committed two of the offenses for which he was presently incarcerated. He says he raped the first victim described above and stole $800 from her. He claims that they had known each other for sometime and she was a "drug dealer." He reports that he stole the automobile, stating, "It was a fair exchange, the police confiscated mine."

He explains that he was first sent to a juvenile correctional facility at age 16 "for stealing automobiles." He states that he was released approximately six months later and he was returned to the juvenile correctional facility within approximately four months for auto theft. He received a 1-10 year sentence in 1965 for theft. His records indicate that he was paroled in January of 1969, violated parole in September of 1970, and was again paroled in November of 1971. His records also indicate that he was arrested for aggravated assault in 1970 (no disposition shown), and for attempted rape and armed robbery in May of 1972 (no disposition shown). He describes his use of alcohol as "light" and does not report illegal drug usage other than marijuana and "experimentation."

Additional Social History: A psychiatric evaluation written in 1975, relates the following: During the interview, he presented himself as a pleasant and polite person of possible average intelligence. He shows no psychotic symptoms of any kind. He does not complain of any psychiatric symptoms. He shows no remorse for his offense and tries to minimize it. He seems to be an anti-social personality and, as such, he is immature, impulsive, and has difficulties tolerating frustration.

He describes himself as "easy going, likable, not hard to get along with. I've never had any clashes except with the Police Department."

He does not report receiving vocational training prior to incarceration. He says he has attended college for four years since incarcerated. He explains that he completed the requirements for an Associate of Arts Degree in December of 1975, and asserts that he will receive a Bachelor's Degree later this year. He has expressed an interest in working in the area of rehabilitation or counseling.

According to this inmate, he completed ten years of school prior to incarceration. He says he received a GED in 1967 at Mid-State.

He reports that he was married in 1969 and divorced in 1973. He does not report fathering children. He states that he corresponds regularly with his ex-wife who presently resides in-state. Likewise, he relates that he corresponds regularly with his parents who reside in-state.

When released he plans to continue college at a nearby university and explains that he was accepted in graduate school in October of 1975.

Case #427

Offense: **Sentence:**

Armed Robbery   6-12 Yrs.

Interviewed: 1976   **Birthdate:** 1947   **Race:** Black

Most Recently Admitted to the Correctional Environment: 1973

Criminal History: This inmate plead not guilty to the offense for which he is presently incarcerated. He was convicted by a jury verdict. His records indicate that he committed armed robbery, in that he took property ($89.85), from a person while armed with a pistol.

This inmate stated that he was only standing in a liquor store when a masked gunman walked in and robbed the liquor store. He asserts that he did not participate in the robbery but says he knew the identity of the armed robber.

This inmate states that he was first arrested at age 10 or 12

76

for running away from home and burglary, and was subsequently sent to a juvenile correctional facility. He indicates that he was released and returned to juvenile facilities regularly for committing offenses such as burglary until age 18. He was arrested for theft in 1966 and escaped. He was arrested again for theft (under $150) in November of 1966 and received 90 days. He paid a fine for trespassing on private property and disorderly conduct in 1967. He was arrested for robbery in 1968 (no disposition shown), and he received a sentence of 1-3 years for burglary in October of 1969.

He describes his use of alcohol as "very light" and reports experimentation with illegal drugs (primarily "speed").

Additional Social History: This inmate states that before he was incarcerated for the present offense he was primarily concerned with stealing and getting "high." He further states, "Now I've realized that's not where it's at." During the interview he was polite and cooperative.

He reports obtaining experience as a bricklayer, steel foundry worker, and shoe maker and repairman prior to incarceration. He states that he has received approximately 2½ years experience as a shoe repairman since incarcerated. He indicates that he is primarily interested in shoe repair.

According to this inmate, he completed nine years of school prior to incarceration. He relates that he attempted to acquire a GED in 1974, but "got bored and quit."

He does not report marrying, but relates that he has fathered one child (born in 1969). He reports that the child presently resides with his (the child's) mother in-state. This inmate states that his mother and father are presently deceased. He says he corresponds regularly with his grandmother.

He indicates that he has been trying to become involved in a group counseling program. He says he plans to pursue the occupational area of shoe repair when released from the penitentiary.

Case #428

Offense: **Sentence:**

Deviate Sexual Assault   30-50 Yrs.
Deviate Sexual Assault   30-50 Yrs.
Aggravated Battery   3 Yrs. 4 Mos. to 10 Yrs.
Unlawful Restraint   1-3 Yrs.
Intimidation ⎫   3 Yrs. 4 Mos. to 10 Yrs.
Intimidation ⎭

(All sentences ordered to run concurrent)

Interviewed: 1976   **Birthdate:** 1947   **Race:** White

Most Recently Admitted to the Correctional Environment: 1973

Criminal History: This inmate plead not guilty to the offenses for which he is presently incarcerated. In November of 1973, this inmate was found guilty by a jury verdict of the offenses of deviate sexual assault, aggravated battery, unlawful restraint, and intimidation.

This inmate was paroled in April of 1973, after serving approximately five years of a 5-20 year sentence for indecent liberties with a child received in April of 1968. He committed the six offenses for which he is presently incarcerated less than five months after he was paroled on a 5-20 year sentence for indecent liberties with a child. His old sentence of 5-20 years has been aggregated with his new sentences resulting in a total aggregated sentence of 35-70 years. His Parole Board date is listed as February of 1981.

His records reveal the following: one day in August of 1973, the victim (a young woman) was in the downtown area of a small town with two friends and in their company visited a number of taverns. At sometime after midnight she had a few drinks with this inmate. That was the second time during the evening that she saw him. After ordering a pizza and calling a cab the two of them proceeded to her apartment since the bars were closing. She intended to call a neighbor to come over, but before she did so she was attacked by this inmate. He started by suggesting intercourse. The victim attempted to brush off his suggestion and tried to get him to return downstairs. At that point this inmate grabbed her by the neck and drug her to the bedroom. He forcibly removed her clothing, tearing her bra in the process. He struck her and prevented her from leaving the bedroom. He committed the first act of deviate sexual assault when he forced his penis into her mouth and down her throat causing her to gag and vomit. When that assault had ended he forcibly led her to a closet where she obtained Vaseline at his request. Then he took her back to the bedroom and he completed disrobing. He then mounted her in a reverse position pinning her arms down with his legs. He then rubbed Vaseline all over his hands and jammed both or one of them into her vagina causing her extreme pain. The rip which he created in her vagina was 9 inches long, and at the time of the operation she had lost three pints of blood.

After this inmate had completed this offense he then proceeded to push the victim's head into a pillow, not allowing her to breathe until she raised her body so as to allow him to have anal intercourse. He forcibly inserted his penis into her rectum thereby committing another deviate sexual assault. When he had completed this act he forced her to get a wash cloth and wash the blood off of him. He then had her call a cab for him and while he waited for the cab he ate some of the remaining pizza. Before he left he told the victim that if she told anyone about the attack he would come back and do the same thing to her and to her children. This constituted the first intimidation offense. He then told the victim that if she told anyone about the attacks he would bring 20 men into court to swear they had gone to bed with her. That constituted the second intimidation offense. Throughout the attack this inmate restrained the victim against her will thereby committing the offense of unlawful restraint. This inmate made no statements or admissions prior to trial and did not testify during the trial. Apart from the reprehensible conduct constituting these six offenses, it should also be noted that after he had caused the grave injury to the victim's vagina, he laughed. His casual departure from the scene by cab preceded by his consumption of pizza appears to have been extremely cruel and ruthless under the circumstances.

Approximately 63 exhibits were utilized at the trial. Many of them illustrated the amount of blood lost by the victim on the bedding and towels. When this inmate was arrested a few hours after the attack, his clothes were removed. On his slacks and undershorts blood was found. Some blood was also found on his shoe. The blood on the defendant's slacks matched the blood type of the victim. Also, a comparison between the pubic hair of the victim and a hair found on the defendant's clothing showed that they exhibited similar characteristics. Fibers taken from the defendant's socks were also similar to fibers in the rug at the victim's apartment.

Although this inmate's prior conviction was for indecent liberties with a child, at the time of that trial he was acquitted of a charge of rape. In addition, prior to the charges of indecent liberties with a child and rape he was convicted of rape, but the conviction was reversed on appeal and he was never retried.

This inmate denies any knowledge of the above-mentioned offenses. His records indicate that he was arrested for violation of probation in August of 1964, at age 16, and was sent to a juvenile correctional facility. He was arrested again in October of 1965, charged with burglary and acquitted by a jury in January of 1966. He was arrested and charged with burglary in March of 1966, was cleared and released.

Materials received from the county State's Attorney's office reveal that in June of 1967 this inmate was tried by a jury and was found guilty of the offense of rape. In August of 1967 a hearing on mitigation and aggravation was held and the court sentenced this inmate to a term of not less than 4 nor more than 12 years in the state penitentiary. Additional documents from county authorities reveal that he was indicted by a Grand Jury in October of 1967, for one count of rape and two counts of indecent liberties with a child. He was reportedly tried by a jury in January of 1968, and was found not guilty of the offense of rape but was found guilty of the offense of indecent liberties with a child. He subsequently received a sentence of 10-20 years for the offense, said offense to be served consecutively with his previous sentence of 4-12 years for rape received in 1967. This inmate's records further indicate that effective February 20, 1969, the sentence of 4-12 years for rape was reversed and remanded to the Circuit Court for a new trial, in that jury instruction had been inadequate in the first trial. In addition, at the same time the Court annulled the consecutive sentence and changed it to read 5-20 years.

In addition to the official history above, this inmate reports that he was first arrested at approximately age 15 or 16 for breaking and entering. He states that as a result of the offense he received probation. He reports that he was sent to a juvenile correctional facility at approximately age 16 or 17 for breaking and entering and asserts that he served 11 months at said facility. He also reports that he was arrested for assault and battery in 1965 and tells that he received 90 days in jail for the offense.

Additional Social History: This inmate states that he was born in-state and reared by his mother. He explains that his mother and father were divorced when he was approximately three or four years old. A psychiatric report written in January of 1974 relates the following: at age 13, he was sent to a juvenile correctional facility for incorrigibility, curfew violations, stealing, receiving a two year incarceration. He ran away from the first juvenile correctional facility and was sent to a second juvenile facility for burglary and breaking into a tavern for money. He remained at the juvenile facility for 11 months and was paroled to his mother's custody. His parole was almost violated when he was arrested for burglary, but the charge was dismissed and he completed parole in 1965. He comes from a single parent family in that his father left the home when this inmate was five years of age. His mother did not remarry. He is fourth youngest of 11 siblings, the oldest is a half-brother, the result of his mother's previous marriage.

According to this inmate, he completed seven years of school prior to incarceration. He reports acquiring an eighth grade diploma at Mid-State in 1969 or 1970. He tells that he has not presently completed a GED and that he is not presently interested in such.

He reports receiving a little experience in construction and

81

home improvement prior to incarceration. He does not report receiving any vocational training at Mid-State. He says he is primarily interested in construction work.

A Pre-Sentence Investigation Report written in December of 1973 relates the following information: his first contact with the probation office was in July of 1959 when he and several other boys were involved in going into an unoccupied home. They were brought to the probation office by the City Police, but no official action was taken. He was officially brought before the Judge in June of 1961 when he was involved in the theft of some beer, money, and other items from drive-in stands. His probation was revoked and in September of 1964 he was sent to a juvenile correctional facility (charge of burglary). He was paroled from the juvenile facility in May of 1965.

The Pre-Sentence Investigation Report continues: on Wednesday evening, December 5, 1973, I went to the county jail to complete the Pre-Sentence Report for this man. However, he did not want to answer any questions, and even after it was explained that this was a pre-sentence report and that he would not have to give any information that he felt would be harmful to him, he stated that if I wanted to know anything, I could get it from the county as all his records were there. He stated that the Judge could take this report and "put it in his pipe and smoke it."

A psychiatric report written in January of 1974 related that this inmate does not have any evidence of formal mental illness. He is alert, clear, and in good contact. He is without need for mental treatment and without mental deficiency. He does not classify as a Sexually Dangerous Person at this particular time. He represents an inadequate personality with sexually aggressive features. The report also indicates that he has a "serious drinking problem." During the interview this inmate described himself as a "heavy drinker" but did not report illegal drug usage.

Apparently this inmate has the interpersonal skills to acquire one of the better job assignments in the correctional environment, i.e., "runner" for the Assistant Warden of Operations. In view of his criminal history, his adjustment to the correctional environment, and his ability to obtain security reductions and positions of status and significant monetary rewards (within the correctional system) is truly amazing. He has only received one disciplinary ticket (for disregarding orders) since his return from a minimum security correctional center in February of 1972. His records indicate that he was returned from the minimum security correctional center because he, along with three other inmates, were caught on the premises of the institutional complex associating with female civilians and in possession of alcoholic beverages.

During the interview, he described himself stating "I get along with people, just about everybody — never hurt anyone at all, ya know."

According to this inmate, he has never committed a sex offense and he is unable to offer any substantial reasons for his criminal history of sex offenses. However, he did indicate that the small rural community in which he lived is probably responsible for his present incarceration, in that he had a reputation as a sex offender. Thus, he asserts that he plans to leave the state after his release from the correctional system.

He relates that he is not interested in "group counseling" stating, "I'm just shy I don't like being around a group." When questioned regarding program involvement, he explained that he acquired an 8th grade diploma at Mid-State in 1969 or 1970, and related that he had not completed a GED. He further stated that he was not interested in acquiring a GED. In addition, he does not report receiving any vocational training since incarcerated. When asked what his primary vocational interest was, he responded, "Construction."

A professional report written in February of 1973 indicates, prior to his last parole board hearing, this inmate attended the Alcoholics Anonymous program at a minimum security unit and also had frequent counseling contacts at Mid-State prior to being transferred to the minimum security unit. Since his return to Mid-State, he has not participated in any organized programs such as Alcoholics Anonymous. However, a vote sheet dated December 26, 1975, indicates "Good program participation." I contacted the Chaplain in charge of the alcohol abuse program at Mid-State and sought information regarding this inmate's involvement. The Chaplain informed me that this inmate was a member in his alcohol abuse program in the past but that he "quit sometime in 1974", and is not presently involved in the alcohol abuse program at Mid-State. During the interview, this inmate proudly announced that he helped start the Lifer's organization in December of 1974 and that he is presently a member of Lifer's Inc. (a self-serving organization which requires a 20 year minimum sentence for proposed membership).

In summary, this inmate is a 30 year-old recidivist sex offender presently serving an aggregated sentence of 35-70 years for indecent liberties, deviate sexual assault (two counts), aggravated battery, unlawful restraint, and intimidation (two counts). Although the Official Statement of Facts relates a particularly brutal sexual assault, police reports included in this inmate's master file indicate additional cruelty. For example, a Police Report written in August of 1973, related the contents of an interview with the victim and reads as follows: During this time, the victim stated that this inmate still held on to her neck with his arm. She stated that he forced her back into her bedroom; threw her down on the bed again and put the Vaseline all over his hands and then he put his legs on the top of both of her arms and he was backwards-like. The victim said that his head was facing her feet and his feet were by her head and this inmate took his hands and jammed them (both hands together) all the way up her vagina); and she said she knew that his hands, while up her vagina were up past his wrists, and he started twisting his hands, while up in her body, and started pulling on her insides and started laughing. The victim said that she screamed and she stated that his laugh was a "horrible laugh." She said that as she screamed, he started hitting her in the head. She stated that he told her that if she made another sound she would be dead. At this time, the victim stated that this inmate had his hand under her chin and also on her throat. She stated that he threatened to kill her several times and kept strangling her. She stated that it was during this attack with his hands up in her body that she started hemorrhaging. The victim stated that the blood gushed from her body — that although the room was dark, she could feel it gushing everything and everywhere.

The victim also stated that this inmate then turned her body somehow and her face was stuck in her pillow on her bed and the pillow was suffocating her. At this time, she stated that he shoved his penis into her rectum. She stated that he kept yelling at her to say dirty things to him and she said that by this time, she could hardly talk or move. The victim stated that this inmate called her names, like "dirty bitch." She also stated that he said, "Damn it — you're going to." The victim stated that she could not remember all of the dirty names that he called her and that he wanted her to call him. She stated that while he still had his arms around her throat and his penis in her rectum; he ordered her to get up on her knees and hunchback like a dog to him; that she better do it or he would kill her. The victim stated that she remembered telling him, "No" and she kept trying to get away. However, he continued to strangle her and by this time, she stated that she could hardly speak. The victim stated that this inmate started to beat her in the head again and she started to black out. She stated that he continued to smother her in the pillow, strangle her with his arms, and threaten her life. The victim stated that she begged for air and finally decided it was hopeless to fight anymore and just remained in the position and prayed that it soon would be over.

Case #429

Offense:	Sentence:
Murder	40-60 Yrs.
Murder	40-60 Yrs.

(Sentences ordered to run concurrent)

Interviewed: 1976   **Birthdate:** 1946   **Race:** White

Most Recently Admitted to the Correctional Environment: 1968

Criminal History: This inmate was found guilty in a bench trial of murdering two men with a .22 pistol outside a lounge at approximately 3 a.m. He claims that he was so drunk at the time of the offense that it took him three days to sober up enough to know he was in jail. He reports that he was incarcerated as a juvenile in Arkansas (six months) for auto theft in 1961, and Iowa (23 months) for breaking and entering (larceny in the night time) in 1964. It is further reported that he received 30 days in jail for resisting arrest in 1966. He was also arrested for assault and battery in 1967 (no disposition shown). He describes his use of alcohol prior to incarceration as "excessive" but does not report using illegal drugs.

Additional Social History: He describes himself as a hard worker and explains that he treats people the way they treat him. During our discussion he stated, "I loved to fight when I was younger, there was nothing I liked better than a good fist fight." He asserts that he has now become more easy going and the past enjoyment associated with fist fights has diminished appreciably. During the interview, he presented himself as relaxed, polite, and good natured.

He states that he gets along "real well" in the correctional environment. However, he is presently in "C" grade for insolence.

He explained that he drove a truck and worked as a roofer prior to incarceration. He asserts that he enjoys physical work and being outside. He says he has received "a little welding training" while at Mid-State but explains "that's about all."

He tells that he completed seven years of school prior to incarceration. He states that he received a GED at Mid-State Penitentiary in 1969 or 1970. He reports that he enrolled in the college program at Mid-State one semester but dropped out without completing a single course.

He explains that he was married in 1966 and divorced in 1967. One child (female) resulted from the marriage and she reportedly lives in an adoption home in an adjacent state. He says his ex-wife lives in Indiana, and they presently correspond. He also reports corresponding on a regular basis with his mother in Arizona as well as his father and sister in Iowa.

Case #430

Offense: **Sentence:**

Murder   Life
Murder   Life

(Sentences ordered to run consecutive)

Interviewed: 1976   **Birthdate:** 1944   **Race:** White

Most Recently Admitted to the Correctional Environment: 1960

Criminal History: Although this inmate plead not guilty to the offenses for which he is presently incarcerated, he explains that he did in fact commit the murders and he was never quite sure why his attorney kept advising him to plead not guilty, unless it was for publicity purposes. He received a separate trial for each offense and was found guilty by jury verdicts in both cases.

His records reveal that the first murder occurred during the armed robbery of a grocery store and the second during the armed robbery of a service station. The first victim was an 80 year-old man, the second was a 64 year-old man. One of the murder convictions was discharged in 1972 after he had been granted parole for the offense in 1971, although he remained incarcerated and began serving his second life sentence. He will be eligible for parole in 1981 or 1982.

' This inmate was made a ward of the court in 1956, at age 12, and placed in an orphanage. He explains that he was arrested at age 9 and again at age 11 for arson. His records report that his mother stated that he also set fire to a cottage at age four because he wanted to see the fire engines arrive.

He relates that he was sent to a juvenile facility at age 14, after he was arrested for burglary. He was released in 1960. Interestingly, this inmate killed two people during the commission of two armed robberies less than eight weeks after he was released from a juvenile facility. When questioned

87

regarding his use of alcohol prior to incarceration, he stated that he had only been drunk on two occasions in his life. He does not report illegal drug usage.

Additional Social History: This inmate describes himself as, "kind of moody — grouchy occasionally, sometimes I'm hard to get along with; sometimes I get reflective and don't want to be around people and get a little snappy." During the interview, he stated that he never really had to "hustle" since he has been incarcerated since age 16. He says he is not really interested in anything and comments, "I don't have any skills, drives, or ambition. I just follow lines. Your life's set for you here, you don't have to do anything." He further stated, "I guess the absence of responsibility is the main thing."

In reviewing this inmate's criminal history, it should be noted that since age 14, he has spent less than 8 weeks in the "free community." He is presently 32 years old and his lackadaisical attitude is viewed as reflective of the fact that he has matured in "correctional facilities." Prior to incarceration, his behavior could be termed sociopathic. However, at this point in time, he seems to present himself as the epitome of an institutionalized individual.

According to this inmate, he did not receive any vocational training prior to incarceration, in that he was only 16 when he began serving his present sentence. Since incarcerated, he reports receiving clerical experience and "a little" vocational training in the area of printing. However, he stated, "I've just never been interested in anything."

He relates that he completed nine years of school prior to incarceration. He states that he received a GED in 1965, and that he has presently completed between one and two years of college. He explains that he dropped out of college during the fall semester of 1975 because he "just lost interest." He further indicates that he has not decided on a major area of concentration but says he will probably return to college.

He does not report fathering children or ever having been married. He tells that his mother is deceased and his father is remarried. He reports that he corresponds with his father on a regular basis and that his father visits him on occasion although it has been three or four years since his father's last visit.

He asserts that he is not interested in group counseling because the members of such groups are overly concerned with presenting themselves in such a way as to please the counselor. As mentioned earlier, this inmate appears lackadaisical, lacking interests and motivation. However, he does not present a lachrymose appearance. In fact, during our discussion, he was surprisingly cheerful and good-humored as well as extremely polite and cooperative.

Case #431

Offense: **Sentence:**

Unlawful Use of Weapons   3-10 Yrs.

Interviewed: 1976   **Birthdate:** 1944   **Race:** White

Most Recently Admitted to the Correctional Environment: 1972

Criminal History: This inmate was found guilty of "unlawful use of weapons" in a bench trial. His records reveal the following: one day in May of 1970 at 10:30 p.m. two police officers on routine patrol curbed the vehicle this inmate was driving because the rear license plate was obstructed. As one of the officers was talking to this inmate, he observed a bulge in this inmate's left front pocket. This inmate stated that the bulge was shotgun shells. The second officer observed one of this inmate's accomplices passing a pistol from the front seat to the back seat. A search of the automobile and the persons in the vehicle uncovered the following: one set of ignition hot wires, two sawed-off shotguns, 18 rounds of shotgun ammunition, two hunting knives, two revolvers and 20 rounds of ammunition, one pair of rubber gloves, four stocking masks and one hard hat. It was also noted that this inmate and two of his accomplices were wearing two sets of clothing.

This inmate was arrested for larceny of a motor vehicle in

October of 1961 (no disposition shown); held for investigation later the same month in a different city (no disposition shown); arrested for contributing to the sexual delinquency of a minor in July of 1963 (no disposition shown); arrested in Louisville, Kentucky as a fugitive in December of 1963 (no disposition shown); received 2-5 years for burglary and larceny in February of 1964; arrested for unlawful use of weapons in November of 1969 (no disposition shown); arrested for unlawful use of weapons (the present offense) in May of 1970; arrested for possession of burglary tools in April of 1971 (no disposition shown); arrested for forgery in November of 1971 (no disposition shown); arrested for murder in January of 1972 (no disposition shown); and his records also indicate that he was arrested for "deceptive practice" (no disposition shown) in September of 1972.

In addition to the official history above, this inmate reports that he was arrested approximately six times as a juvenile for car theft, burglary, larceny and robbery. He relates that he was sent to a juvenile correctional facility in 1959 for interstate transportation of a stolen automobile. He states that he was released from the juvenile facility in June of 1961. He says he has been arrested in approximately 15 different states for offenses such as being drunk and disorderly, disorderly conduct, speeding, and drag racing. He comments that he received a sentence of 2-5 years for burglary and larceny in 1964. He says he was discharged in March of 1968. As reported earlier, he committed the offense for which he is presently incarcerated in 1970. He explains that he was arrested for possession of burglary tools in 1971 and says he believes he received a sentence of six months supervision. He also commented that he was arrested on January 20, 1972, for murder, asserting, "I beat it March 1, 1972." In addition to the above, he received two concurrent 18 month to 5 year sentences for forgery in June of 1972. His records indicate that both forgery sentences were discharged in December of 1975.

Additional Social History: A psychiatric report written in October of 1971, relates the following: He had difficulties in his adjustments, particularly with his father who was a quiet man but never at home; and he felt that his mother was very

90

protective and he felt for the first 14 years of his life that he was looked upon as a weakling. He experienced many physical complaints as a child and was not permitted to step beyond the front door of his house. He felt that he had to observe all his friends playing and talking but his mother would not permit him to leave the house. He feels that he was put in many positions where he was deprived of his childhood. He felt that the kids were making fun of him. He was a weak boy and he was having many problems. At the age of 14 when he recuperated from his upper respiratory infections and other infections which almost crippled him, he began getting more involved but at that time he began to commit criminal acts. Over-all during my interview (psychiatrist's interview) it became apparent that we are having here a very severely disturbed man who has been reacting strongly to the weak physical situation he has been having plus the strong rebellious angry feeling he has experienced for a strong domineering woman being the mother and the very difficult relation and feeling for his father who was almost non-existent.

During our discussion, this inmate explained that he was married in 1970 and divorced in 1974. He states that one child (female) resulted from the union and that the child presently resides with his ex-wife. He says he does not know where his ex-wife and child presently reside. He reports last seeing his wife in 1974.

According to this inmate he completed nine years of school prior to incarceration. He reports acquiring a GED at Mid-State in 1965. He asserts that he has presently completed over two years of college. He says he received an Associate of Arts Degree in psychology in 1966. He also claims he only needs 14 semester hours to complete requirements for a Bachelor's Degree.

He reports receiving experience as a motorcycle and auto mechanic, diesel mechanic, heavy equipment operator, plumber, carpenter, welder, steamfitter, and truck driver prior to incarceration. He says he is primarily interested in construction. It's interesting to note that according to materials contained in his master file, his three accomplices involved in the offense for which he is presently incarcerated were black. However, a report included in his master file, dated March, 1975, authored by the clinical services supervisor relates that this inmate was seen wearing a swastika on a chain around his neck. He has also been reportedly identified by staff members as agitating black inmates. Whenever there are problems of a racial nature, he assumes a leadership role. When racial tension is high he is always observed leading his line to the assignment in the Clothing House. He is reported as hating blacks and stating that he hates blacks in the cellhouse. The same report indicates that he "has also had severe disciplinary problems at two Northern prisons. Several of his misconducts have involved threats to kill correctional officers (guards).

When asked about his threat to kill a staff member this inmate commented that he has a big mouth and that he really didn't mean it, but he gets angry and he feels he has to do something to calm down.

His records indicate that he is an ordained minister of the Church of the New Song and he explains that the administration is misinterpreting what he is doing. He says his religion is trying to unite people, and avoid the existence of gangs and racial differences, but the administration accuses him of the opposite, i.e., hating blacks and being one of the causes of the racial disturbances.

This inmate is considered to be a disciplinary problem and has had two years statutory good time revoked. He has received nine disciplinary tickets in the past six months for offenses such as insolence, improper conduct, improper language (committing mutinous acts of inciting to riot), disregarding orders, and giving false information to an officer.

When questioned regarding alcohol usage prior to incarceration, this inmate indicated that he regularly consumed large quantities of ethyl alcohol. He stated that he generally drank three cases of rum and half a dozen cases of wine per week. When questioned regarding illegal drug usage, he related that he used "about all of them" and he asserts that he "burned up a vein" in his arm shooting cocaine. He states that he has used heroin and morphine since age 15 but denies ever having been addicted. He says he mixed six drugs together on one occasion and almost died. He comments that he has been in a "coma condition" on three separate occasions as a result of drug usage. He claims that he is "down" on drug users because

92

they are weak and the "only thing I'm a^f slave to is my Harley."

This inmate appears fairly articulate and intelligent. During our discussion he took great pride in explaining that he had jumped a moving car with his motorcycle without the benefit of a ramp. Needless to say, he was physically injured as the result of said accomplishment. He reports that he rode with motorcycle gangs for approximately three years before being incarcerated in 1964. He says he returned as a motorcycle gang member after his release from prison in 1968 and continued said activity until his incarceration in 1972. During the interview, he asserted, "I'm gonna ride that motorcycle 'til the day I die." He tells that he enjoys riding "bikes" more than anything else, although he says his "biggest goal" is to drive in the Daytona 500 before he dies. He tells that he enjoys any kind of motor racing competition and states, "I'm a 32 year-old kid. I don't want to grow up. I enjoy my life, I'm satisfied." He says he has quit smoking and has decided to cut "way down" on drinking and 90% of his drug usage. He says the only thing he'll "use " now is "speed" or marijuana. He describes himself stating, "Unique, invincible, diabolical and cynical, and fabulous." He further commented, "I treat people the way I like to be treated. I'm a convict. I don't dig that resident bullshit."

He reports that he fought in Golden Gloves boxing competition as a juvenile (middle weight division). He states, "I just like to laugh and joke and do my time." However, he explains that he has had numerous fights and that he assaulted an officer in a Northern prison in October of 1972. He also explains that he assaulted an Assistant Warden in the psychiatric division in 1967. He says he was in the psychiatric division from May of 1967 to March of 1968. He states that he has been studying law for ten years and asserts that he is as good as 85% of the attorneys on the street. He also commented during our discussion that he would be out of prison in 60 days.

Case #432

Offense: **Sentence:**

Murder   17-25 Yrs.

Interviewed: 1976   **Birthdate:** 1944   **Race:** Black

Most Recently Admitted to the Correctional Environment: 1967

Criminal History: This inmate plead not guilty to the offense for which he is presently incarcerated. He was convicted by a jury verdict. His records reveal the following: One day in August of 1966, this inmate sexually assaulted and killed "a small boy" with a hunting knife. The murder was apparently a rather gruesome affair. This inmate's residence was located by following a trail of blood from the boy's dead body, which was discovered in an alley. The police reports reveal that this inmate's home contained numerous blood stains as well as a blood stained hunting knife. Although police reports indicate that this inmate admitted the fatal stabbing of the victim, during the interview this inmate stated that he did not kill the boy and he did not know who did.

This inmate explains that he was first arrested at age 13 for stabbing another adolescent with a knife. He says because of the offense, he served two years in an out-of-state juvenile facility. He also received a 60 day jail sentence for criminal damage to property in April of 1965.

Additional Social History: During the interview, this inmate described himself as a "lady of the opposite sex." He states that he has "never had a woman." He indicates that he enjoys having sex with men of his choice and that he is not interested in sexual contacts with women. This inmate also views himself as a good-natured counselor. He says he tries to help other people and neglects himself but he always comes out on "the short end of the stick." However, at the present time he seems

94

to be quite satisfied with his role as a "lady of the opposite sex."

He explains that during his lengthy period of incarceration, he has been sexually assaulted and forced to submit to homosexual demands on three different occasions by black gang members. In spite of past difficulties, he indicates that he is not having unusual difficulties adjusting to the correctional environment at the present time.

He explains that he did not possess any vocational skills prior to incarceration. He further explains that he has not acquired any vocational skills since incarcerated. He has expressed an interest in counseling as an occupation.

According to this inmate, he completed seven years of school prior to incarceration. He tells that he is presently involved in the GED program.

He does not report ever having been married or fathering children. He states that his parents are deceased; his mother died when he was born; his father died when he was approximately three years-old; and his step-mother died when he was 22 years-old.

When questioned regarding release plans, this inmate stated, "I would like to open up a place to help peoples."

Case #433

Offense: **Sentence:**

Armed Robbery   20-60 Yrs.

Interviewed: 1976   **Birthdate:** 1944   **Race:** White

Most Recently Admitted to the Correctional Environment: 1973

Criminal History: This inmate plead guilty to the offense for which he is presently incarcerated. His records reveal the following: One day in January of 1973, this inmate entered a private residence armed with a .38 caliber revolver and a nine millimeter pistol. He threatened the residents (a married couple and their daughter) and forced the husband to open his safe. This inmate then took approximately $3,000.00 from the victims. He was apprehended at the scene by city police officers. He explains that he was having financial difficulties and that "friends" told him the victims' residence would be a good place to rob because they had "a lot" of money. He says he feels his friends "set him up" because the police were waiting for him.

He claims that he was first arrested at age thirteen for stealing "a couple bottles of pop" and was sent to juvenile correctional facilities in Georgia. He states that he was released approximately one year later but was returned to juvenile facilities for a couple of months because, as he remembers it, he ran away from home. He received a twelve month sentence for burglary in Georgia in 1960, and a fifteen month sentence for burglary in 1962 in Georgia. He says he was arrested for vagrancy in Tennessee in 1965 and his records reveal he was arrested in Illinois in 1967 for improper parking and illegal possession of weapons (no disposition shown). He explains that he was arrested and convicted of assault with intent to commit murder in Iowa in 1967 (after police attempted to arrest him for speeding and he tried to shoot their tires out with a pistol so as to avoid paying a fine). His records indicate that he received a sentence of thirty years for assault with intent to commit murder in February of 1967. He received parole for the offense in March of 1972. He describes his use of alcohol as "fairly light" and reports "light experimentation" with illegal drugs.

Additional Social History: He describes his health as "damaged" and asserts that an oven exploded at a Northern State Penitentiary in 1975 when he tried to light it. He says he was burned severely and that 40% of his body was covered with third degree burns. He also comments that he has had trouble with his nerves since the accident.

In years past, he has attempted suicide in the following ways: hanging himself, taking sleeping pills, cutting his wrists, and he has also drunk acid. When questioned regarding enemies, this inmate asserted that "Black Peace Stone" gang members were his enemies because he would not go along with their protection rackets, and he indicates that he has received sex pressure from "Black Peace Stone" gang members while incarcerated in the East Cell House. He presently resides in the South Cell House and he comments that he "gets along all right" in the South Cell House if he watches where he goes. He has expressed an interest in transferring to another, smaller penitentiary.

He reports receiving vocational training as a cook and baker prior to incarceration. Since he was burned, he asserts that he is too "heat sensitive" to continue cooking or baking.

According to this inmate, he completed five years of school prior to incarceration. He states that he received a high school diploma at a Mcn's Reformatory in 1970. He also relates that he has currently completed six college courses and that he plans to continue in the college program.

He does not report ever having been married or fathering children. He tells that he corresponds regularly with his mother and father who reside in an adjacent state.

This inmate asserts that he was "extensively involved" in group counseling and in the Jaycees while incarcerated in Iowa. He claims he has been unable to "get into" anything here. He has expressed an interest in group counseling and joining Lifer's, Inc.

Case #434

Offense: **Sentence:**

Murder   40-70 Yrs.

Interviewed: 1976   **Birthdate:** 1943   **Race:** White

Most Recently Admitted to the Correctional Environment: 1966

97

Criminal History: This inmate plead not guilty to the offense for which he is incarcerated. The Official Statement of Facts indicates that he left a tavern between 1:00 and 1:30 a.m. with a thirty-six year old female acquaintance and her body was subsequently found in an alley a short distance from the tavern. The woman's clothes had been removed except for a shirt, and death was attributed to multiple stab wounds in and about the body. He states that he did not do "it" ten years ago, and asserts that the fact of the matter is he did not; and if it means not making a parole which he apparently wants very badly, he insists, "I cannot admit to something I did not do."

He reports that he was incarcerated in a boys' home as a juvenile for suspicion of burglary. His records indicate an arrest in 1960 for theft over $50.00 (no disposition shown), for drunkenness in 1962 (no disposition shown), rape in 1963 (no disposition shown), driving while intoxicated in 1964 (no disposition shown), and battery in 1965 for which he served six months in a state farm. He tells that he was prone to "get drunk on occasion" prior to incarceration. He does not report using illegal drugs.

Additional Social History: During the interview he stated, "I was kind of bitter when I came in. For a while I was a little bitter but now I got it practically all in." He further states, "I treat people as they treat me. I don't get violent. I'm good humored. I came in with a chip on my shoulder but I started looking at the way it was and not the way I wanted it to be." During our discussion he was friendly and polite.

According to this inmate, he worked as a baker, a laborer, a cook, a busboy, and as a carpenter prior to incarceration. Since incarcerated he asserts that he has received experience in cooking, painting, and heavy equipment operation. He presently works in the Water Filter Plant. He says he is primarily interested in heavy equipment operation.

He states that he quit school in the seventh grade because he kept failing. He further states that his English was so poor when he first entered Mid-State Penitentiary that he could not carry on a conversation in English. He indicates that he came from a Spanish speaking neighborhood in Texas and has learned English for the most part while incarcerated. He tells that he received an eighth grade diploma at Mid-State in 1967 or 1968.

He reports that he was married in 1961 and separated in 1963. He says the separation was his fault because he was young and "just liked to run around a lot." He states that two children resulted from the union and that they presently reside with his wife in Texas. During our discussion he commented that he has not seen his wife in eleven years.

He explains that his father has a job for him in Texas, in the area of construction and heavy equipment operation.

Case #435

Offense: **Sentence:**

Murder   75-125 Yrs.

Interviewed: 1976   **Birthdate:** 1943   **Race:** White

Most Recently Admitted to the Correctional Environment: 1965

Criminal History: This inmate plead not guilty to the offense for which he is presently incarcerated. This inmate, together with his stepmother's brother, shot and killed the victim of the offense. The killing was the result of an agreement between the men mentioned above and the father of this inmate. This inmate's father was to pay them the sum of $300 for killing the victim, who had allegedly been carrying on a romance with the wife of this inmate's father.

His records indicate that he was committed to a juvenile correctional facility at age 14 for auto theft. He escaped after approximately one week and was then sent to a second juvenile correctional facility where he remained for six months. He was again sent to a juvenile facility at age 15 as a juvenile parole violator after he was apprehended drunk while driving a car. He was released from the juvenile facility seven months later.

This inmate was then sentenced to a state farm at age 20, for "theft of a spare tire and battery while drunk." He was released four months later. He describes his use of alcohol as "moderate" although he does admit to occasional intoxication on weekends. He does not report illegal drug usage.

Additional Social History: During the interview, he stated, "While I'm here, I do my own time." He explains that he does not have the patience for reading. However, he says he likes to read novels and science fiction if they have "a lot of action." He says he likes books that describe "a lot of fighting," e.g., a gunfight. He describes himself as "easy going."

He reports that prior to incarceration, he had received experience in the areas of auto mechanics, automotive body work, and machine operations. He states that he has not received any vocational training since incercerated. He comments, "It just doesn't interest me." However, during our discussion, he did indicate that he had learned typing and other clerical skills since incarcerated.

He tells that he completed eight years of school prior to incarceration. He says he has failed the GED qualifying exam on two separate occasions. He explains that it is necessary to pass the qualifying exam prior to taking the GED exam.

He states that he was married in 1960 or 1961 and divorced in 1964. According to this inmate, two children resulted from the marriage (both female). He says he does not know where his daughters presently reside. He asserts that his father is incarcerated in the Department of Corrections serving a sentence of 150 years for murder. He indicates that he corresponds with his mother who is presently remarried and that she visits on a regular basis.

When questioned regarding release plans, he stated, "I don't know, it's hard to say — I don't plan on comin' back to jail." He has expressed an interest in work release which he feels would afford him an opportunity to acquire employment.

Case #436

Offense: **Sentence:**

Burglary   20-40 Yrs.

Interviewed: 1976   **Birthdate:** 1943   **Race:** White

Most Recently Admitted to the Correctional Environment: 1963

Criminal History: This inmate plead guilty to the offense for which he is presently incarcerated in that he and two 17 year-old accomplices burglarized a grocery store. He received three years probation for the offense in September of 1963. His records describe a rather long and sordid affair which resulted in the revocation of his probation. His probation was revoked after a series of criminal offenses were committed by this inmate and an accomplice, including forcing two teenage girls (one age 13 and one age 16) to accompany them in their car while they periodically had intercourse with the girls, swapping sexual partners, and threatening the girls with pistols.

This inmate has an arrest record dating back to age 15. In 1958, he was charged with theft, and was placed in the custody of a juvenile correctional facility. He spent approximately five years at two different juvenile facilities. It's reported that he was paroled and subsequently returned for parole violations on two separate occasions, once for car theft and the second time for writing bad checks. In 1963, he was fined $300 for disorderly conduct and assault and was remanded to the County Jail in lieu of payment of fines.

During the interview, he stated that he had only been arrested on two occasions prior to the present offense, i.e., approximately age 16 for burglary and approximately age 18 for an additional burglary. He states that he does not drink or use illegal drugs.

Additional Social History: He tells that he presently has "a lot of problems with his people." The difficulty according to the subject of this report involves the recent death of his father, his mother's present mental attitude, and the recent nervous breakdown of one of his brothers. During the interview, he appeared extremely defensive and preoccupied with other concerns. He revealed limited verbal ability but asserted that he could get a job tomorrow if released.

He states that he has had training in the areas of electricity and plumbing. He says he has received no formal training but has learned it on his own. He explains that he has experience as a gaffer on a chair line — building chairs. He also reports that he has experience in the area of shoe repair and asserts that he is primarily interested in shoe repair.

This inmate tells that he completed eight years of school and says he has attended school intermittently since incarcerated. He reports that he reads and writes a little, stating, "I can make out with my reading."

He indicates that he has never married. He explains that his father died in 1975, and that his mother presently resides instate. According to this inmate, he has three brothers and four sisters. He says he corresponds regularly with his mother and intermittently with his younger sister.

When questioned regarding release plans, he indicated that he planned to live in North Carolina and work in his uncle's furniture factory.

Case #437

Offense: **Sentence:**

Murder   Life

Interviewed: 1976   **Birthdate:** 1941   **Race:** White

Most Recently Admitted to the Correctional Environment: 1961

Criminal History: This inmate plead guilty to the offense for which he is presently incarcerated. His records indicate that he became involved in an argument over some trivial matter with his sixty-two year-old landlady. He apparently made a rather vicious assault upon her with a wrench and knife, beating and stabbing her to death. Then he attempted to place her body in a furnace. His records also indicate that he had been drinking heavily prior to the assault. During the interview, he stated that he just went "insane."

He explains that he was incarcerated as a juvenile for Burglary and Forgery. He tells that he was incarcerated at a work farm for 120 days in 1959 for unlawful use of an automobile. He states that he was sentenced to a colony farm (chain gang) in Georgia on two occasions — receiving a six month sentence for public drunkenness on a highway, and a twelve month sentence for simple larceny in the early 1960's. His records further reveal that he left junior high school and was sent to a juvenile correctional facility on a charge of forgery. He was paroled, violated parole, and was sent to another juvenile facility at age fifteen. At age seventeen he was paroled to the chief of police in Middletown and worked an office job at the city police department for approximately six months. However, he lost his job when he stole some money and the car of the chief of police. He was then sent to a state work farm. He describes his use of alcohol as "heavy" and denies illegal drug usage.

Additional Social History: When asked to describe himself, he stated, "I'd say extrovertive, sociable, good at verbal or written communication." During the interview, he was pleasant and friendly and appeared fairly well adjusted to his present environment.

He was diagnosed in 1961 as follows: Basically a delinquently motivated, sociopathic personality who in spite of repeated admissions to correctional environments, has failed to profit by such experiences. He clearly knows and recognizes that his actions in the past and in the present are contrary to accepted standards of living, and knows the difference between right and wrong. Thus, we are dealing with an adolescent, who has never grown up to accept responsibility in the free community. It is felt that the problem has been complicated by alcohol, and by his having few ties of a constructive nature. He has turned against those administrative officials who have tried to help him. While he expresses remorse for losing his temper and aggressiveness in the past to the degree that the life of a person was taken, it is more providence than restraint that has prevented similar occurrences in the past. It is to be expected that he will reflect an adolescent temperament when frustrated. It is further expected that he will be extremely friendly and helpful to those persons viewed as having some capacity to alleviate his incarceration.

He explains that he completed the heavy equipment training program at Mid-State in 1973. He tells that he has had intermittent training in the areas of library science, watch repair, refrigerating and heating, typing, and accounting. He has expressed a primary interest in refrigerating and air conditioning.

According to this inmate, he completed nine years of school prior to incarceration, received a GED at Mid-State in 1963, and has completed forty-five quarter hours of college and two quarter hours of vocational counseling at Mid-State.

He indicates that he was married at age nineteen and divorced approximately three months later in that the marriage was annulled. He tells that his father died when he (this inmate) was two years old. He says he has never met his mother and was reared by an aunt and uncle. He further states that he corresponds regularly with a brother.

Case #438

Offense: **Sentence:**

Theft   1 Yr.
Transportation and Possession of Alcoholic
Liquor, Sales to a Minor, Contributing to the
Delinquency of a Minor, and Unlawful Use of

Weapons	1 Yr.
Criminal Damage to Property	1 Yr.
Escape	3-9 Yrs.
Burglary	3-9 Yrs.
Theft	3-9 Yrs.
Theft Exceeding $150 in Value	3-9 Yrs.
Escape	3-9 Yrs.
Escape	3-9 Yrs.
Aggravated Assault	1 Yr.

(All sentences ordered to run concurrent)

Interviewed: 1976   **Birthdate:** 1939   **Race:** White

Most Recently Admitted to the Correctional Environment: 1973

Criminal History: This inmate plead guilty to the offenses for which he is presently incarcerated. His records reveal the following: This inmate was arrested in June of 1973, in the company of an accomplice and two juveniles. The arrest was made by a State Trooper for a minor traffic infraction. Upon approaching the car, the trooper observed this inmate making a suspicious move. The trooper made all of the occupants of the car get out and he found a loaded .38 revolver in the glove compartment of the automobile. He also discovered a quantity of opened and unopened liquor and what was later proven to be various stolen articles. It was also later discovered that the automobile was stolen.

In June of 1973, this inmate and his accomplice escaped from the county jail, but they were recaptured within a few hours.

In July of 1973, this inmate and his accomplice again escaped from the county jail and were recaptured approximately four days later. While at large, this inmate and his accomplice robbed a post office.

In August of 1973, this inmate and his accomplice again escaped from jail and were at large for approximately three days before they were recaptured.

Between the time of the original arrest and sentencing, the states of Kentucky, Ohio, Connecticut, Massachusetts, Nebraska, and Colorado all responded to inquiries concerning this inmate and his accomplice. However, extradition papers were not forthcoming.

This inmate explains that he was sent to an orphanage at age 6 or 7, then to a juvenile correctional facility at age eight for "not going to school, running away from home, etc." He received a sentence of one year to age in connection with an auto theft in 1957. He states that he was released from juvenile correctional facilities in Ohio at age 20. Shortly after his release he committed two burglaries and received two concurrent 1-15 year sentences for burglary in 1960. Materials received from the Ohio parole authorities reveal the following: This inmate was admitted to an Ohio State Reformatory in March of 1960, to serve 1-15 years for the crime of burglary (two concurrent). He was paroled in February of 1962; declared a parole violator at large March 1, 1963; restored to parole March 29, 1963; declared a parole violator June 21, 1963; returned June 27, 1963. He was reparoled on September 17, 1964; declared a parole violator at large November 13, 1964; returned August 19, 1966; declared an escapee June 4, 1967; returned January 14, 1970; reparoled October 21, 1971; and declared a parole violator at large January 21, 1972.

He also received a two year sentence for violation of the Dyer Act in 1964 and a three year sentence for housebreaking in Kentucky in 1967. He describes his use of alcohol as "very little" and does not report illegal drug usage.

Additional Social History: During the interview, this inmate explained that he had been "locked up" for 28 years of his life and when he has been released in the past he has just wanted to "break loose." He describes himself as "easy-going."

This inmate reports that while incarcerated over the past three decades, he has received experience in the areas of landscaping, painting, cooking, building maintenance, nursing, and as a florist. He also adds that he has worked in the laundry since his arrival at Mid-State Penitentiary.

According to this inmate, he completed eight years of school prior to incarceration. He says he has become involved in educational programs at different correctional facilities, but to date has not acquired a GED. He tells that he is not presently interested in acquiring a GED.

He explains that he was married in May of 1972 and that he

and his wife separated when he was arrested for the present offense. During our discussion he commented, ''I've been trying to get a divorce ever since.'' He relates that his wife is presently a Lieutenant in the Army, resides in California, and recently filed for a divorce.

When questioned regarding release plans, this inmate stated, ''I'm planning on getting married in July if my divorce comes through.'' He says he plans to marry a nurse. He reports that his intended bride has three children and that he plans to work in a hospital laundry and help support them.

==

Case #439

Offense: **Sentence:**

Armed Robbery   30-60 Yrs.
Attempted Escape   1-3 Yrs.

(sentences ordered to run consecutive)

Interviewed: 1976   **Birthdate:** 1931   **Race:** White

Most Recently Admitted to the Correctional Environment: 1966

Criminal History: This inmate plead not guilty to the offense of armed robbery for which he is presently incarcerated. Legal materials indicate that he robbed a jewelry store while armed with a ''gun.'' He was found guilty of attempting to escape from a Northern state penitentiary in 1973. Initially he was convicted of four counts of armed robbery, having plead guilty to three of the charges for which he received three sentences of 10-15 years to run concurrent with each other as well as the fourth sentence of 30-60 years. The three 10-15 year sentences were discharged in 1973. He has a three page FBI fact sheet dating back to 1946 which indicates that he has been incarcerated in the past for auto larceny as a juvenile; assault with intent to commit murder, auto larceny, and armed robbery as an adult. He received five 10-20 year sentences for five counts of armed robbery in 1956. After being paroled in 1964, he was arrested less than four months later and subsequently convicted of four additional armed robberies. He describes his use of alcohol as moderate and denies illegal drug usage.

Additional Social History: During the interview, he presented himself as intelligent and articulate. During our discussion, he was polite and well mannered. He is viewed as an extremely sophisticated manipulator.

He explains that he "gets along well" at Mid-State. As mentioned earlier, he attempted to escape from a Northern prison in 1973. Materials included in this inmate's Master file reveal that the escape attempt was an extremely sophisticated one involving a great deal of planning and forethought.

He explains that prior to incarceration, he did not possess any vocational skills. However, since incarcerated, he reports that he has become a registered barber and has acquired a great deal of experience in plumbing and clerical work. He states that he is primarily interested in rehabilitation counseling and working as a counselor.

He tells that he completed eight years of school prior to incarceration. According to this inmate he received a GED at a Northern State Penitentiary in 1953. He relates that he has approximately 31 hours of college and is presently in the college program at Mid-State. He says he would like to ultimately receive a Bachelor's Degree and acquire a position as a counselor.

He reports that he has never been married. He states that he corresponds regularly with his mother in Ohio and an aunt in California. He further indicates that his father is deceased.

Case #440

Offense: **Sentence:**

Indecent Liberties with Child   6-15 Yrs.
Indecent Liberties with Child   1 Yr.
(Sentences ordered to run concurrent)
Interviewed: 1976   **Birthdate:** 1929   **Race:** White

Most Recently Admitted to the Correctional Environment: 1970

Criminal History: This inmate entered a plea of guilty to Indecent Liberties in that he engaged in sexual intercourse with a seven year old girl and her nine year old sister. At the time of the offense the children were living in the same household as this inmate.

The seven year-old girl and her nine year-old sister were questioned after this inmate was arrested and their version of the facts was substantively identical in that this inmate repeatedly, over the course of a number of months, had sexual intercourse with each of them on a regular basis. They stated that the acts of intercourse were performed in the presence of each other and two other adult men. One of the men testified at the hearing in aggravation and mitigation that he was present on at least two occasions when this inmate had intercourse with the seven year-old girl. The doctor's testimony at the hearing and in his report to the State's Attorney's office indicated that the children had been sexually abused, resulting in vaginal scarring.

This inmate has a long and sordid history of criminal offenses dating back to 1939. When he was nine years old and in second grade he appeared before a judge for tampering with a motor vehicle. Eight weeks later, he was arrested for stealing toy guns from a department store and was arrested a third time for stealing jewelry within two months of the second arrest. He was arrested numerous times at age ten for stealing from local stores, stealing from parked cars, and attempting to steal a truck. Also, at age ten, he was sent to a juvenile correctional facility for boys. He was returned home in December of 1941 and returned to a juvenile facility as a juvenile parole violator in 1943 after stealing a bicycle.

109

Shortly after his second release from juvenile correctional facilities, he stole an automobile and burglarized a service station. He was found guilty of larceny of a motor vehicle in 1946, and at the age of sixteen, was sentenced to serve four to ten years in the state penitentiary. The burglary charges were subsequently dropped.

This inmate was released from prison in 1951 and again arrested in 1958 for burglary. However, the charge of burglary was reduced to possession of stolen property to which he plead guilty, asked for and was granted three yeas probation. After violating probation less than four months later, he received a sentence of one to three years which he served at Mid-State Penitentiary. He was convicted of contributing to the sexual delinquency of a child in 1962 and received a one year prison sentence.

Additional Social History: During the interview, this inmate described himself as, "antisocial as hell — I have no use for people and don't want people around me. Inside and out, I've had nothing but a pack of liars around me. People make me sick. I don't think it's much different on the outside." He asserts that most people are crooked and states, "I don't want nothing to do with anyone — I want to be left alone." During our discussion he further commented, "A criminal mind or an insane person doesn't trust doctors or lawyers." This inmate made the following statement with reference to the present offenses, "The more you educate a child when they are young, the quicker they form their own ideas, like sex, they need to learn."

This inmate presented himself as extremely defensive and bitter regarding his present incarceration. He charges, "They've been playing games with me ever since I got here."

He does not report having enemies at this or any other correctional facility in the state.

He explains that he was a "handyman" and did general maintenance such as treetopping, yard work, carpentry, plumbing, and electrical work prior to incarceration. He does not report receiving any vocational training since incarcerated.

Most of this inmate's formal education was in grade schools. He reportedly had "problems" in all of them and subsequently didn't learn much. His records indicate that he quit school at age 21; he was enrolled in ninth grade at the time.

According to this inmate he was married in 1955 and divorced in 1969. He states that two children resulted from the marriage. He says he was married a second time in 1970 and although his wife gave birth to a child shortly after their marriage, he asserts that "it" is not his but his wife's brother's. He reports that his wife was sent to a state mental hospital in 1971 and indicates that he does not know where she resides at the present time, nor does he care. His records indicate that he has fathered numerous children in and out of wedlock and has lived with numerous women.

When questioned regarding his release plans, this inmate stated, "I feel that's my business." He further commented, "I plan to get a job and go off some place by myself."

Case #441

Offense:	Sentence:
Armed Robbery	50-75 Yrs.
Armed Robbery	50-75 Yrs.
Kidnapping	1 Yr.
Kidnapping	1 Yr.
Assault with Intent to Murder	1-14 Yrs.

(The above sentences were ordered to run concurrent)

Robbery	10-20 Yrs.

(Ordered to run consecutive to the 5 sentences listed above)

Assault with Intent to Murder	10-14 Yrs.
Assault with Intent to Rob	1-14 Yrs.
Kidnapping	1 Yr.

(Ordered to run concurrently with each other but consecutively to the
10-20 year sentence received for robbery)

(At this point in time all sentences have been aggregated to a total of 70-109 years.)

Interviewed: 1975   **Birthdate:** 1925   **Race:** Black

Most Recently Admitted to the Correctional Environment: 1955

Criminal History: This inmate plead guilty to the nine offenses listed above. His records indicate that all of the above charges were related to raping and attempting to rape white women.

His records indicate that he has a long history of violations of the law. At age 12, he was sentenced to a juvenile correctional facility but he escaped from that facility and other juvenile institutions at least five times. When he was 17 years old, he was sentenced to a pentitentiary for not less than 10 nor more than 25 years for armed robbery. After he was paroled on that sentence, he was arrested for sodomy and carrying a concealed weapon, at which time he was delcared a criminal sexual psychopath and sentenced as such. He escaped in 1955, and while at large, he raped a white woman and robbed her and her companion. In escaping the last time, which was the first part of 1955, he attempted to cut a jail attendant's throat with a broken Coke bottle.

He describes his use of alcohol as "social" and denies illegal drug usage.

Additional Social History: During the interview, this inmate spoke incoherently at times and had a tendency to ramble speaking rapidly and asserting that he had advanced training in chemistry "organic, not inorganic", agriculture, horticulture, nursing, printing press operations, general maintenance, etc., in an obvious attempt to impress upon the interviewer that he was in fact a learned man. He would make statements, such as, "ecology is, of course, related to things which change their nature and composure which is related to a composition of changes" and then he would skip to another subject and make similar statements. When asked if he was interested in additional education in any of the areas of study he mentioned, he stated he was too busy to become involved in an educational program. While talking with this inmate, it became apparent

112

that he was more interested in impressing the interviewer than with offering candid information regarding his past training, interests, or future plans. His responses appear to offer insight into his personality regarding his felt need for approval and respect.

He states that he gets along very well in the institution. He explains that he presently works on a sanitation crew inside the institution and says he enjoys the work.

He states that he completed elementary school and later received a GED around 1949. The lack of information offered as to specifically where he received a GED causes one to doubt that he in fact completed a GED.

He states that he has never been married. He explains that he corresponds regularly with "quite a few" relatives — primarily with a sister in an adjacent state.

======

Case #442

Offense: **Sentence:**

Aggravated Kidnapping   25-50 Yrs.

Interviewed: 1976   **Birthdate:** 1922   **Race:** White

Most Recently Admitted to the Correctional Environment: 1966

Criminal History: This inmate plead guilty to the offense for which he is presently incarcerated. His records reveal that at about 3:30 p.m. one afternoon in November of 1965, he abducted a five year old girl as she was returning from school. The young girl was found approximately two hours later in his car. He had raped her and the young girl suffered severe lacerations and bruises and also suffered from shock. In connection with the above, this inmate was initially charged with aggravated kidnapping, rape, and indecent liberties with a child.

113

His records indicate that he was incarcerated from 1948 to 1958 in a California penitentiary for "lewd and lascivious" conduct, in that he attempted to sexually assault a seven year old girl in the women's restroom of a grade school. It is noted that he was paroled in 1953 and violated parole the same year. His records further indicate that he was involved in an escape attempt from prison in 1955.

He received a one to three year sentence in Arizona in 1962 for Indecent Exposure; was arrested for drunkenness in 1964; and arrested for criminal damage to property in 1965. When questioned regarding his consumption of alcohol prior to incarceration, he stated, "Whenever I get to drinking, it'd be too much — I'd go off on a binge for two or three months at a time." He states that he has never used illegal drugs.

In view of this inmate's history of aggressive sexual molestation of young girls, it is interesting to note that a psychiatric evaluation written in 1966, reveals that he was the passive partner in acts of anal intercourse at age nine or ten; and further reveals that he reported being raped at age fourteen or fifteen while incarcerated in a correctional facility.

Additional Social History: This inmate has consistently argued that his problem is excessive alcohol consumption. The fact that he refuses to deal with sexual behavior and/or motivation for such is most unfortunate. During the interview, he described himself as quiet and easy-going.

His records indicate that he has never received a disciplinary ticket. He does not report having enemies at this or any other correctional facility.

He tells that he worked as a construction laborer, longshoreman, and truck driver prior to incarceration. He states that he has not received any vocational training in the past nine years. He further states, "I'm not really much interested in anything anymore. The reason I don't get involved in programs is they can't seem to do anything around here without making a mess out of it."

He explains that he completed eleven years of school. He states that he took the GED exam in a California penitentiary in approximately 1953, but claims that they would not give him a GED certificate because he had a bad conduct discharge from the armed services. He says he is not interested in acquiring a GED and states "education doesn't mean anything to me."

During the interview, he denied ever having been married. However, a clinical report included in his records reveals that he was married in 1944 to a woman who was nineteen years of age. He lived with her for seven months and was then sent overseas. When he returned in 1946, he found that she was living with another man. They were divorced later during the same year. During our discussion, he explained that his parents were deceased and asserted "I do not have any family."

V
Young First Offenders: Their Criminal Careers (Part II)

Twenty-three case histories (17% of the original sample) will be presented in this section. They were selected for presentation because they represent some of the more comprehensive documented criminal careers of young first offenders presently available. Unfortunately most of the juvenile records for the offenders listed below were either destroyed or inaccessible. As mentioned earlier it is most difficult to construct comprehensive criminal records because of city, county, and state policies which block access to a juvenile's criminal record. The cases which follow are arranged in chronological order.

Case #501

Offense: Armed Robbery   **Sentence:** 5-15 Yrs.

Interviewed: 1976   **Birthdate:** 1956   **Race:** Black

Most Recently Admitted to the Correctional Environment: 1974

Criminal History: This inmate plead not guilty to the offense for which he is presently incarcerated. His records reveal that during the early morning hours, one day in June of 1973, this inmate and two male companions, (while wearing masks over their faces and armed with a sawed-off shotgun) robbed the owners and two patrons of a tavern. During the interview, this inmate stated that he was talked into participating in the robbery by his two accomplices.

He explains that he was first arrested at age 15 for robbery, in that he stole money from a vending machine. He says he received one year probation. His records indicate that he was on juvenile probation from February 8, 1972, until March 27, 1973. His records do not indicate any additional arrests or convictions. When questioned regarding his use of illegal drugs, he stated, "I don't take drugs; I smoked a little marijuana."

Additional Social History: He describes himself as a "somewhat likable person." During our discussion he seemed to be concerned with obtaining a GED as well as additional vocational training. During the interview he was polite and cooperative.

He explains that he had not received any vocational training prior to incarceration. He also asserts that he has not received any vocational training since incarcerated. He states that he is primarily interested in welding and electronics.

According to this inmate, he completed 11 years of school prior to incarceration. He reports that he took the GED exam in February of 1976 but did not pass the exam because he did poorly on the reading comprehension section. He has expressed an interest in college vocational courses after completing the GED.

He does not report ever having been married or fathering children. He states that he was living with his parents when arrested for the present offense. He tells that he corresponds regularly with his parents and that they visit him on occasion. He says he has six brothers and two sisters.

Case #502

Offense:	Sentence:
Attempted Murder	25-75 Yrs.
Aggravated Kidnapping	10-30 Yrs.
Rape	15-45 Yrs.
Attempted Murder	25-75 Yrs.
Attempted Murder	25-75 Yrs.
Aggravated Kidnapping	25-75 Yrs.
Aggravated Kidnapping	25-75 Yrs.
Rape	25-75 Yrs.
Aggravated Battery	25-75 Yrs.

(All sentences ordered to run concurrent)

Interviewed: 1976   **Birthdate:** 1954   **Race:** Black

Most Recently Admitted to the Correctional Environment: 1974

Criminal History: This inmate plead guilty to the offenses for which he is presently incarcerated. He was convicted in a bench trial. The Official Statement of Facts reveals that one day in July of 1973 this inmate, armed with a pistol, abducted a young woman in an urban area, drove her to an isolated area, raped her, then drove to a park, raped her a second time, then choked her and threw her into a lagoon in the park. The victim regained consciousness while in the water and this inmate

119

assisted her in extricating herself whereupon she recognized him as her attacker and at that time he started beating her with a sharp instrument inflicting a scalp wound and fracturing her arm. The victim eluded him by retreating into the water where she remained until this inmate left the area. This inmate voluntarily confessed to the aforementioned offenses and a motion to suppress his confession was denied.

In addition to the above offenses, this inmate was indicted for a murder committed in April of 1973. This inmate abducted and took a young woman to the same park, referred to above, where he raped her, choked her and threw her body into the lagoon. Several days later, the woman's body was found floating in the lagoon. After this inmate's arrest in the aforementioned case, and while confessing he reportedly voluntarily confessed to the murder.

This inmate relates that he was first arrested at age fourteen for petty theft and was released to his parents. He states that he was arrested six or seven times as a juvenile for petty theft. His FBI Fact Sheet indicates that he was arrested in August of 1971 for disorderly conduct and criminal trespass (no disposition shown). A Pre-Sentence Investigation Report indicates that he was fined $100 and costs for theft in May of 1972.

His records further reveal: one day in June of 1972 this inmate was charged with rape, deviate sexual assault, aggravated battery and attempted murder and in January of 1973 he was sentenced to six months at a state penal farm on the battery charge in that case. The female victim in that case had been raped while in her apartment, forced to submit to a deviate sexual assault, stabbed in the abdomen, choked into unconsciousness and the gas jets of the kitchen stove were left open. This inmate was only convicted of battery in connection with the aforementioned offenses. He describes his use of alcohol as "social" and does not report illegal drug usage.

Additional Social History: This inmate relates that he was incarcerated in the Mid-State Psychiatric Division for approximately nine months in 1974. A Psychiatric report written in February of 1974 states that this inmate was oriented and in contact but spoke in a very low voice and appeared depressed.

He verbalized regret over past happenings and claimed he could not sleep for thinking about them. He talked quite freely about his attempt to rape his mother, which was unsuccessful when she slapped him. He reported hearing voices, usually one of the victims who calls his name or asks him to help her. This is in the way of a distant, rather loud hallucinatory experience and occurs during the daytime when he is not occupied. Occasionally, he also hears his girlfriend's voice. However, none of these auditory sensations ever suggested doing anything of an aggressive nature, such as sexual assaults. A Psychiatric evaluation written in September of 1974 asserts that this inmate has a personality structure that (in view of our present knowledge and understanding today) does not lend itself to the average methods of treatment useful in neurosis, minor character disorders, and even in certain types of affective phychoses.

During the interview, this inmate described himself as "nice," "quiet," and "easy to get along with." He does not report having specific enemies at this or any other correctional facility. He further indicates that he is not having unusual difficulties adjusting to the correctional environment at the present time. During our discussion, he informed the author that he has been a member of the "Disciples" for six years. An Institutional Transfer Report written in November of 1974 relates that he was segregated from the inmate population for a short while for congregating with alleged gang members in a suspicious manner. His records also indicate that he has received five disciplinary tickets in the last year and one-half.

This inmate reports receiving training in sheetmetal working, welding, woodworking, and a little carpentry. He says he received sheetmetal and welding training at a Northern State Penitentiary and drafting training at Mid-State. He states that he is primarily interested in architecture.

According to this inmate, he completed ten years of school prior to incarceration. He reports receiving a GED at Mid-State in 1976 and tells that he is presently enrolled in college classes.

Previous professional reports indicate that this inmate's parents were not married. In 1969 he formed a commonlaw relationship and lived with a woman from 1970 to 1973. He explains that the woman had two children from a previous relationship and that he also fathered a child with the woman. He reports that the woman and her children presently reside in-state. He also commented that he had not corresponded with the mother of his child in approximately two months.

Case #503

Offense: **Sentence:**

Burglary   1½-6 Yrs.

Interviewed: 1976   **Birthdate:** 1954   **Race:** White

Most Recently Admitted to the Correctional Environment: 1973

Criminal History: This inmate plead guilty to the offense for which he is presently incarcerated. His records reveal the following: One evening in November of 1972, this inmate broke into the V.F.W. post in a small city, and tried to steal a quantity of liquor and some money. He was observed in the premises by local officers who arrested him on the scene. The County State's Attorney described this inmate stating that he fits the classic image of the "punk," rejecting any guidance from anyone except contemporaries with the same attitude. He dropped out of both school and society for the same reason, he was unwilling to work hard enough to be a decent human being. His prior convictions include resisting arrests, drinking as a minor, criminal damage to property, and misuse of license.

He was paroled from Mid-State Penitentiary in May of 1974, and was returned to prison within months. While on parole he was involved in a tavern fight, arrested for aggravated battery, and paid a fine for disorderly conduct.

He states that he was first arrested at age twelve for "disorderly conduct or something." He asserts that he was arrested on numerous occasions as a juvenile for offenses related to alcohol. He was fined $50.00 and received six months probation for disorderly conduct in 1971, at age seventeen. He was again arrested for disorderly conduct in 1972 (no disposition shown). He relates that his FBI Fact Sheet is not comprehensive in that he has been arrested numerous times as an adult for offenses related to excessive alcohol consumption. During the interview, he indicated that he was an alcoholic and although he does not report using illegal drugs, drug abuse is strongly suspected.

Additional Social History: During the interview, this inmate stated, "My dad was a drunk, so I drank. What do you expect?" He asserts that his father was an alcoholic and drank every day for over twenty years. With reference to his father, he further commented, "He was in and out of A.A. hospitals." During our discussion, this inmate also commented, "I'm a loner. I like to stay by myself most of the time."

He has a long and sordid history of alcohol abuse. He lacks motivation and tells that he is not interested in learning a vocational skill and only plans to do "as little as possible." He also informed this interviewer, during a rather candid conversation, that he would probably be drinking alcohol within an hour of his release from prison. He says he "goes crazy" when he drinks whiskey and may scream and yell or break out windows. However, he does report that he has been a member of Alcoholics Anonymous for approximately one year and is presently a member.

He asserts that he did not receive any vocational training prior to incarceration. He also asserts that he has not received any vocational training since incarceration. He states that he is primarily interested in "nothing" but "for the record" indicated that he was interested in building.

According to this inmate he completed seven years of school prior to incarceration. He relates that he has not been involved in any educational programs since incarcerated becaue he is not interested in them.

He does not report ever having been married or fathering children. He states that his father died in 1975. He says he corresponds regularly with his mother who presently resides in-state. When released he says he plans to live with his mother and seek employment, "anything I can get."

Case #504

Offense: **Sentence:**

Armed Robbery   8-24 Yrs.

Interviewed: 1976   **Birthdate:** 1953   **Race:** Black

Most Recently Admitted to the Correctional Environment: 1974

Criminal History: This inmate plead guilty to the offense for which he is presently incarcerated. The Official Statement of Facts reveals the following: one day in June of 1973 this inmate and two male accomplices robbed a tavern. During the robbery this inmate placed a shotgun to the head of the owner and demanded that all persons in the tavern lie on the floor of the building. Money was taken from five people in the tavern. All three robbers were masked during the commission of the crime.

Approximately one week later this inmate admitted to a police officer during questioning that he robbed the tavern. He also identified his accomplices, one of whom was his brother. Later a written statement was made by this inmate admitting the crime and admitting specifically that he was the individual who carried the shotgun.

This inmate reports that he was first arrested at age 17 for fighting, and subsequently served 30 days in jail. He states that he was arrested a second time at age 18 for auto theft in Louisiana for which he received a three year prison sentence in 1971. In June of 1972, he was convicted of unauthorized use of an automobile, contributing to the delinquency of a minor, and theft. His records indicate that he received a $500.00 fine and costs or six months in jail on each of the three counts. When questioned regarding his use of alcohol, this inmate stated, "I don't drink." Likewise, he does not report illegal drug usage.

Additional Social History: Psychiatric evaluations written in 1974 reveal the following: this inmate has a long history of

124

anti-social behavior dating back to childhood. He argued considerably with other children. He quit school in the 7th grade at age 13. He says he can read and write a little bit. He states that he made good grades but would not pay attention to the teacher and thus was expelled. He stole a car at age 13, and began "significant fighting" at age 17. He enlisted in the Air Force and served six months, but received an undesirable discharge because he sexually molested a young man. He claims he was discharged from the service because a fellow soldier claimed that he (this inmate) attempted to have sexual relations with him. However, he denies any homosexual activity. Since incarcerated he says, his mind "comes and goes." He says he does things and doesn't remember doing them, i.e., "jumping" his father prior to being jailed.

This inmate states that he has experimented with drugs in the past, primarily marijuana. He does not report ever having been addicted. He claims that his mind "goes" and he tells that occasionally he hears voices, i.e., people talking but he can't make out what they are saying.

During the interview, this inmate commented, "When I did the auto theft I was young, understanding was zero. I was just messing around. I didn't have my own car." He further stated, "This armed robbery — I was influenced and was high on white port wine." During our discussion, he described himself stating, "I'm not hard to get along with."

This inmate does not report having specific enemies at this or any other correctional facility in the State at the present time. He reports that he has been a member of the "Disciples" since 1967 or 1968. However, he asserts that he is a member of a different branch of the "Disciples" than those here at Mid-State from "up North." He relates that he received sex pressure in 1974 from another Disciple at Mid-State. However, he reports that his membership in the "Disciples" organization is now recognized in this state and he is no longer having difficulties in this regard. He further indicates that he is not presently having unusual difficulties adjusting to the correctional environment. Perhaps it should be mentioned that this inmate has received numerous disciplinary tickets in recent years and has received seven such tickets this year resulting in Segregation placement in April of this year.

125

He reports receiving auto body repair experience at a program funded by Job Corps when he was 17 years old. He does not report receiving any vocational training since incarcerated. His records reveal that he has been placed in Segregation or on an unassigned gallery since August 18, 1975. However, prior to August of 1975, he had been placed in Segregation on numerous occasions for offenses such as fighting, improper conduct, disobeying orders, and causing a disturbance. He complains that he is "locked up" all the time when he would prefer to have a job assignment. He says he is primarily interested in truck driving.

According to this inmate, he completed seven years of school prior to incarceration. He reports attending school at Mid-State since 1975. He relates that he attends school five days a week, one hour per day. However, he states that he has not acquired an 8th grade diploma as of this date.

He does not report ever having been married or fathering children. He tells that he was born and reared in Louisiana and that he moved in-state and lived with his mother and father approximately three months before his arrest. He says he corresponds with his mother and father who presently reside in Louisiana. This inmate's older brother is also incarcerated at Mid-State, and was his accomplice in the armed robbery for which they are both presently incarcerated.

Case #505

Offense: **Sentence:**

Murder   50-150 Yrs.

Interviewed: 1976   **Birthdate:** 1952   **Race:** Black

Most Recently Admitted to the Correctional Environment: 1973

Criminal History: This inmate plead not guilty to the offense

126

for which he is presently incarcerated. He was convicted by a jury verdict. His records reveal the following: The victim was found beaten and shot to death one day in July of 1973, with two bullet wounds in the back and one in the back of her head. She was discovered along side the road, face down, by a passing motorist. The murder weapon was a .38 caliber pistol, which was found in this inmate's home. A witness saw this inmate with the victim a few minutes before the murder.

His records indicate that he told the following story to a county probation officer in November of 1973: This inmate and a friend were drinking beer and whiskey, and they were inhaling acrylic spray at his friend's home the day and the night of the murder. This inmate saw a girl go past the house. Both men got on their bikes and pursued the girl. This inmate says his friend stopped to talk to the white girl. He asserts that he stayed in the road, his friend on the sidewalk with the girl. He says his friend put his bike down and put his arm around the girl. This inmate also reports that the victim wanted his friend to go to her place and play records and drink and then she "started to hollering." He reports that his friend then began hitting the girl with a gun and the girl "shut up." This inmate claims that his friend was using his (this inmate's) gun. This inmate also asserts that he left the scene because his friend wanted to talk to the girl.

He tells that he was arrested approximately six times as a juvenile for offenses such as "trying to outrun the law in a car" and "burglarizing bicycles." According to county authorities he was first arrested in May of 1969 for theft, and received one year probation in June of 1969, and a $100.00 fine. He was arrested for petty theft in July of 1970 (no disposition shown); aggravated battery in January of 1971 (sentenced to 10 days in county jail); illegal possession of liquor in January of 1971 (fined $25.00 and costs); reckless driving in September of 1972 (fined $100.00 and costs); criminal damage to property in March of 1972 (one year probation, restitution, and court costs); reciprocal non-support in May of 1972 (no disposition shown); and attempted escape (no date, and no disposition). This inmate's county traffic record reveals that he has been fined on numerous occasions for offenses such as reckless driving, attempting to elude police, illegal transportation of liquor, improper lane usage, too fast for conditions, and driving while his license was suspended. When questioned regarding his use of alcohol, he indicated that he drank to excess prior to incarceration. When questioned regarding his use of illegal drugs, he stated, "I smoked some grass, but I didn't use it like I used alcohol." His records indicate that he was placed in segregation and reduced to "B" Grade for possession of a controlled substance in December of 1974.

Additional Social History: During the interview this inmate appeared extremely suspicious and defensive.

He explains that he had not received any vocational training prior to incarceration. Since incarcerated, he states that he has "learned about this Boiler House" and he further comments that he is presently a "turbine operator."

According to this inmate, he completed 11 years of school prior to incarceration. A high school transcript included in his Master Record File reveals that he was enrolled in special education classes (EMH — Educable Mentally Handicapped) while in high school. His records further indicate that he informed the staff psychologist on December 5, 1973, that he could not read or write.

His records indicate that he was married in December of 1970 to a woman who was "pregnant by him at the time" and they were divorced in October of 1972. His records further report that he has one child, born out of wedlock in June of 1973. He states that he married the mother of his second child in 1973 and they presently remain married. He says his wife and child presently reside in-state.

When questioned regarding release plans, he stated, "Not drink for one thing. I do see that that was my problem — drinking."

Case #506

Offense: **Sentence:**

Rape   8-20 Yrs.
Aggravated Kidnapping   8-20 Yrs.
Armed Robbery   8-20 Yrs.

(All sentences ordered to run concurrent)

Interviewed: 1976   **Birthdate:** 1952   **Race:** White

Most Recently Admitted to the Correctional Environment: 1973

Criminal History: This inmate plead guilty to the offenses for which he is presently incarcerated. The Official Statement of Facts reveals the following: at approximately 2:20 a.m. one June day in 1973 a young couple was parked in an automobile on a rural road at which time three assailants drove up in an automobile. One of the assailants remained in the car while this inmate and the other assailant approached the victims' parked car. They robbed the victims of approximately $60.00 at gun point and beat the male victim, striking him on the head with a shotgun. The male victim was then locked in the trunk of his automobile and the female victim was forced into the assailants' automobile. This inmate and his two accomplices drove for a short distance and then this inmate and his accomplices took turns having intercourse with the victim. It is also reported that this inmate attempted to force the girl to suck his penis before they released the victim on a rural road.

The following day one of this inmate's accomplices surrendered himself to a detective of the county sheriff's department and gave a full confession, implicating this inmate as well as the other accomplice. Following their arrests, this inmate and the other accomplice also confessed to the crimes.

During the interview, this inmate stated that he was extremely intoxicated and high from smoking marijuana at the time of the offense and asserted that initially he and his accomplices intended to rob the victims "just for kicks." However, he claims that he did not rape the victim because he could not achieve an erection.

This inmate explains that he was first arrested at age 15 for stealing tires "off an old junk car." He reports that he paid a fine for stealing the tires. He was arrested for burglary in October of 1969. He relates that he subsequently served 86 days in jail and received one year probation. He was arrested in June of 1970 for burglary and received 2½ years probation with the first five months to be served at a work farm. He received a federal sentence of two years for the offense of "interstate transportation of stolen property" in December of 1970. He relates that he was released from a Federal Youth Center in July of 1972. His records report that he was arrested in August of 1972 for disorderly conduct (fighting) and he reports paying a fine of $55.00. When questioned regarding past usage of alcohol, he stated, "I'm in Alcoholics Anonymous right now." He further stated that he drank moderately during the week but would become extremely intoxicated on weekends. He reports light experimentation with illegal drugs and marijuana usage.

Additional Social History: During our discussion, this inmate explained that he was engaged at the time of the present offenses and that such behavior is totally contradictory to his personality. He describes himself as talkative and says "I've stole a few tires and cashed a few bad checks but I'm no 'rapist'." During the interview, he was polite and cooperative.

This inmate reports receiving experience as a machine operator, factory worker, and house builder (carpenter) prior to incarceration. He states that he received carpentry experience from his father who has been a carpenter for 25 years. He relates that he has not received any vocational training since incarcerated. He says he is primarily interested in acquiring his own business in real estate and/or housing.

According to this inmate, he completed ten years of school prior to incarceration. He explains that he took the GED exam last month and is presently waiting for the results. He comments that he has taken the GED exam on two prior occasions but states that he did not really study for the exam on the two prior occasions as he has recently.

He relates that he was born and reared in-state, with the exception of six or seven years when he lived in California. He does not report ever having been married or fathering children. He tells that he was engaged to be married when arrested for the present offenses. He says his fiancee has since married another man.

He relates that he plans to live with his parents when released.

Case #507

Offense: **Sentence:**

Robbery   2-6 Yrs.

Interviewed: 1976   **Birthdate:** 1950   **Race:** White

Most Recently Admitted to the Correctional Environment: 1974

Criminal History: This inmate plead guilty to the offense for which he is presently incarcerated. His records reveal the following: one day in January of 1974, this inmate and an accomplice drove to the rear of a food store at approximately 12:30 a.m. This inmate walked into the store and his accomplice remained in the car. This inmate had a wig on and purchased a loaf of bread and a pack of cigarettes. Then with a starting pistol in his hand, he ordered the clerk to place the money from the cash register in the paper bag containing the bread and cigarettes. He then left the store, got into the car with his accomplice and they drove away. They were apprehended shortly thereafter.

This inmate stated that he first met his accomplice when they were both in the penitentiary. This inmate was arrested for criminal damage to property in 1970. He was first sent to prison in 1971, at which time he received a 1-10 year sentence for theft. He was paroled 9 months later in December of 1971.

131

While on parole he received a second prison sentence of 2-10 years in January of 1972 when he was convicted of theft over $150.00. He was again paroled in October of 1973. Then he was arrested for armed robbery in January of 1974 and he was convicted of robbery in March of 1974 and received his present sentence.

Additional Social History: This inmate reports that he was born and reared in-state. He states that he has two half brothers and one half-sister. He asserts that he does not have a father; the implication being that he was born out of wedlock. He relates that his mother was first married when he was approximately two or three years old and he reports that he hated his mother's husband because he (his mother's husband) "hated me because I wasn't his kid." He also tells that his mother recently married for the fourth time in May of this year.

This inmate's mother reported that he was an "illegitimate child," but he was not aware of it until he was in high school. His mother was first married in 1950 and was divorced ten years later. His mother then married a second time in 1966. The marriage lasted about six weeks. Then his mother was married a third time in December of 1970.

This inmate has a brother, age 21, and a sister, both living at home. He asserts that he also has a brother who escaped from the penitentiary.

This inmate states that he has been a homosexual (he refers to himself as a woman and prefers that others do likewise) since age 11. He explains that he was first "married" at age 19 or 20 and that his "husband" died in a car accident approximately one year later. He tells that he was "married" a second time on September 12, 1975, while incarcerated at Mid-State penitentiary. He reports that correctional officials (guards) are not aware of his marriage, but he asserts that he is presently married. He says his "husband" is presently housed in the segregation unit, although they are cellmates as a rule.

According to this inmate he completed 11 years of school prior to incarceration. A transcript received from the high school he attended, reveals that he only completed ten years of school, in that he withdrew during the 11th year. He reports acquiring a GED in 1973. He also relates that he completed two college courses prior to incarceration. He says he would be interested in attending college while incarcerated if he did not have to live in the East Cellhouse to do so.

He says he received secretarial experience prior to incarceration. He estimates that he types approximately 80 words per minute on a manual typewriter and 95 words per minute on an electric typewriter. He also reports that he is skilled in shorthand. He does not report receiving any vocational training since incarcerated and asserts, "I'm not going to East House to get it either." When asked why, he stated, "Too many blacks, all they can think about is getting their dick wet, and I ain't into that." He tells that he is primarily interested in secretarial work, although he added, "That and being a housewife." He does not report alcohol or drug usage.

It is noted in this inmate's master file that one of the last places he was employed indicated in correspondence dated April of 1974, that he performed his work poorly, and needed continuous supervision. It was also noted that he was "physically weak" and an "odd individual with homosexual tendencies."

This inmate, as related earlier, is a homosexual who views himself as a "woman." During the interview he explained that he was in a "bad mood" because his "husband" had been removed from their cell and placed in the segregation unit for fighting. He claims that he and his "husband" are saving their money in hopes of purchasing a sex change operation for him (this inmate).

This inmate described himself stating, "Intelligent. I've got a mind of my own. I make my own decisions. Quiet until someone messes with me, then I become dirty, lowdown, and just plain nasty." It is interesting to note that correspondence received from his mother in April of 1974, described him as "Easily led" and indicated that he was prone to have temper outbursts and fainting spells.

This inmate does not report having specific enemies at this or any other correctional facility. He complains that he cannot get a security reduction to "minimum" because he is a homosexual. He says he was sent to the psychiatric division in 1971 for protection based on his homosexuality. He explains that he has been a homosexual since age 11 and he does not need to be

133

sent to the psychiatric division for protection.

He tells that when he is released he plans to start a typing service while waiting for his "husband" to be released.

Case #508

Offense: **Sentence:**

Voluntary Manslaughter   6 Yrs. 8 mos.-20 Yrs.

Interviewed: 1976   **Birthdate:** 1950   **Race:** Black

Most Recently Admitted to the Correctional Environment: 1973

Criminal History: This inmate plead guilty to the offense for which he is presently incarcerated. His records reveal that he was initially indicted for five counts of murder. The victims were a twenty-six year old female, a seven year old male, a five year old female, a thirty-five year old male, and a twenty-six year old male. All five victims were found in an apartment located next to this inmate's residence.

During the interview, he stated that he had been target practicing on the day of the murders and that, while armed with his pistol, he entered the victims' apartment through the window and found four dead bodies. He claims that the thirty-five year old victim told him that since he (this inmate) saw the four bodies, he (the thirty-five year old victim) would have to kill him (this inmate) also. This inmate says he and the victim fought over his pistol and that it went off and killed the man. When asked why the thirty-five year old victim did not shoot him as he had allegedly shot the others, this inmate stated that the victim did not have a gun. When asked how the thirty-five year old victim could have shot the others without a gun, this inmate stated, "I don't know."

Interestingly enough, as revealed in police reports, this inmate has told numerous contradictory stories in the past about

134

how the murders occurred. When ballistic reports indicated that all the victims were killed with this inmate's pistol, he told a story about how he had loaned his gun to the thirty-five year old victim prior to the murders.

Police reports also state that all of the bodies were clothed or partially clothed in undergarments, except for the twenty-six year old female who was completely nude, and it was believed that a rape was involved. It is further reported that evidence obtained in the case included the semen stained clothing of this inmate and the clothing of the twenty-six year old female victim.

As a result of plea bargaining, this inmate plead guilty to the voluntary manslaughter of the thirty-five year old victim and the four additional/murder counts were dismissed. He asserts that he plead guilty to the charge of voluntary manslaughter because "the judge" threatened to give him five one hundred year sentences if he plead not guilty.

This inmate states that he was first arrested at approximately age nine in Arkansas for hitting a white woman. He further explains, "She stepped on my foot, told me to get out of her way, and slapped me, so I hit her." He reports that he was held in jail overnight and then released. He relates that the only other time he was arrested, was at approximately age thirteen or fourteen for suspicion of shoplifting (he says he was released the same day). When questioned regarding his use of alcohol, he indicated that he drank every day but he claims that he never became intoxicated. When questioned regarding illegal drug usage, he stated that he tried drugs (mescaline and marijuana) approximately four times.

Additional Social History: He describes himself as "a lone wolf." During the interview, he stated, "I don't like to be around people and talking makes me bored."

He does not report having enemies at this or any other correctional facility in the state. He further indicates that he is not having unusual difficulty adjusting to the correctional environment at the present time. However, during our discussion, he stated that he was a member of the "Metro-East" inmate organization (gang) for self-protection.

He explains that he has been on an unassigned gallery since the early part of 1974. When questioned regarding occupational interests, he stated, "I got too lazy to do anything." He tells that he received a welding certificate and a carpentry (finishing) certificate from Job Corps in Michigan prior to incarceration. He says he is interested in acquiring his own business and perhaps raising hogs.

According to this inmate, he completed nine years of school prior to incarceration. He relates that he has taken the GED exam on three or four occasions, but to date has failed the test every time. He says he enjoys reading comic books. He indicates that he is not presently interested in school because, as he tells it, one hour a day in school will not do him any good as far as preparing for the GED exam.

He reports that he was married in 1971 and is still married to the same woman. He states that two children resulted from the marriage. He further states that he has not corresponded with his wife in approximately ten months. He also claims to have fathered six additional children by other women and he asserts that he "took care" of all the children prior to incarceration.

This inmate stated that he was not interested in group counseling and further commented, "I don't see no use in it. I already know how to deal with my problems, that's why I don't have none now." When questioned regarding release plans, he stated, "Find a business I can go into for myself."

Case #509

Offense: **Sentence:**

Armed Robbery   4-8 Yrs.

Interviewed: 1976   **Birthdate:** 1947   **Race:** Black

Most Recently Admitted to the Correctional Environment: 1973

Criminal History: This inmate plead guilty to the offense for

136

which he is presently incarcerated. His records reveal the following: One day in February of 1968, at approximately 12:30 p.m., this inmate and an accomplice robbed a man in his apartment, in that this inmate pointed a gun at the victim and took from him the sum of $30 in U.S. Currency and an Omega wrist watch (valued at $50). This inmate was arrested the following day at approximately 11 a.m., by police officers answering a burglary call. At the time of arrest this inmate was in possession of a .32 caliber snub nose revolver. The armed robbery victim made a positive identification of this inmate and in May of 1970 this inmate was admitted to probation for five years after pleading guilty to the offense of armed robbery.

In January of 1971, a warrant was issued for this inmate's arrest in that he had never reported to his probation officer as ordered by the court. In addition, in August of 1970 he failed to appear in court to answer to a charge of burglary. Bond was forfeited and a warrant was issued.

In October of 1971, this inmate stole a .357 magnum pistol from the patrol car of a driver's license examiner for the Mississippi Highway Patrol. This inmate was received at Mid-State Penitentiary from a Mississippi State Penitentiary in April of 1973 where he was serving a two year sentence.

This inmate explains that he was first arrested at age 12, but says he does not remember what he was arrested for. He further commented that he was arrested three or four times as a juvenile, once for auto theft and once for the assault and battery of a police officer as well as resisting arrest (he estimates his age at 14 or 15 at the time and states that he does not remember the disposition). He describes his use of alcohol as, "occasional drinker/holiday drinker." He does not report illegal drug usage.

Additional Social History: During the interview, this inmate described himself stating, "I get along with everyone I encounter. I'm a fair guy. I'm not a partier. I don't drink that much."

He does not report receiving any vocational training prior to incarceration. Since incarcerated, he says he has received training in the areas of electricity and electronics. He relates that he has received two certificates in appliance repair, one in

1975 and one in 1976. He also reports receiving a certificate for "Life Skills Development" in 1974 and a certificate in "Career Counseling" in 1975. When questioned regarding his primary vocational interest, he stated, "I'm truly interested in some type of business or other, a clothing store or appliance store."

According to this inmate, he completed ten years of school prior to incarceration. He states that he received a GED in 1974. He comments that he is not interested in college vocational courses.

He explains that he was involved in a common-law marriage from 1964 to 1973. He states that three children resulted from this relationship and that two of the children presently reside with their mother in Mississippi. He relates that the other child lives with his (this inmate's) parents in-state. He also relates that he has not seen his common-law wife since 1973 and that they rarely correspond.

He says he wants to go to a small city and open up a business of "some sort" when released.

======

Case #510

Offense: **Sentence:**

Attempted Rape   2⅓-7 Yrs.

Interviewed: 1976   **Birthdate:** 1947   **Race:** Black

Most Recently Admitted to the Correctional Environment: 1972

Criminal History: This inmate plead not guilty to the offense for which he is presently incarcerated. He was received in 1972, to begin serving a sentence of two to three years for robbery. In 1973, he was transferred to a work release center. While residing at the work release center, he apparently committed a home invasion and attempted rape. His records received from the

138

county reveal that he entered the bedroom of a young woman, grabbed her by the throat, threatened her with bodily harm, undid his trousers and got into bed with her.

He was first arrested in 1964 for theft and received a fine of $500.00. He was arrested for forgery in 1966 and indecent liberties with a child in 1967. He received two years probation for burglary in 1968 and after being arrested for unlawful use of weapons, forgery, and burglary in 1970 (while still on probation), he received a one to three year sentence for burglary. He explains that he was arrested in 1971 for aggravated assault, in that he was accused of assaulting two women (the charge was apparently dropped). His records also indicate that he was arrested for robbery in 1971 and attempted burglary in 1972 before receiving the previously mentioned two to three year sentence for robbery in 1972. He describes his use of alcohol as "social" and does not report illegal drug usage.

Additional Social History: During our discussion, he stated, "My goal in life is to settle down and make a change, anything gets old." He relates that he is bisexual and that he becomes sexually involved with the pseudo-women in the institution. In 1975, his former cellmate attempted to visit him at Mid-State Penitentiary. His former cellmate (who was on parole at the time) came to the prison dressed as a woman and accompanied by this inmate's mother, father, and grandmother. This inmate's mother and grandmother reportedly attested to the fact that the former inmate was this inmate's wife and was in fact a woman. However, a matron who searched the individual in question discovered the visitor who claimed to be a woman was in fact a man, and he was taken into custody.

He reports having received "a little" experience as an auto mechanic prior to incarceration. Since incarcerated, he explains that he received a certificate in meat processing in 1973. He says he is primarily interested in becoming a youth counselor.

According to this inmate, he completed ten years of school prior to incarceration. He has not completed a GED at this point in time and says he "just didn't feel like getting one."

He relates that he was married in 1966 and divorced approximately two months later. He states that he was married a second time in 1968 and divorced in 1972. He reports that two children resulted from the second marriage and that they presently reside in-state with his ex-wife, who is remarried. He asserts that he has also fathered numerous other children by various women.

When released he plans to reside in a half-way house initially. He reports that he presently has a "girlfriend" and may get married a third time.

Case #511

Offense: **Sentence:**

Aggravated Kidnapping   10-25 Yrs.

Interviewed: 1976   **Birthdate:** 1947   **Race:** White

Most Recently Admitted to the Correctional Environment: 1972

Criminal History: This inmate plead not guilty to the offense for which he is presently incarcerated. He was convicted by a jury of the offense of aggravated kidnapping. At the time of the offense this inmate was living out-of-state. His records reveal the following: One evening in August of 1971, this inmate and accomplice abducted a twelve year-old girl from in front of her home and took her by automobile to a deserted country road where this inmate and his accomplice raped her. They left the victim at the scene of the assault and proceeded to drive out of the state. However, they were stopped by a police officer in-state, but they were released when a search of the car failed to reveal the girl who had been released a short time earlier. This inmate and his accomplice were arrested out-of-state a few days thereafter and were later extradited to the state in which he is presently incarcerated. At the trial, this inmate denied involvement in the kidnapping, but admitted that he had been drinking in the area where the offense took place.

At the age of fourteen or fifteen, this inmate received six

months probation in connection with a charge of unlawful entry. At the age of eighteen, he was fined on a charge of malicious destruction of property. In July of 1965, he was granted three years probation on a charge of breaking and entering with the first twelve months to be served in prison camp. In February of 1968, he was sentenced to a term of three to five years for violation of probation. He served two years, seven months on the sentence before he was paroled, but was later returned on a parole violation and served an additional seven months. He was on parole at the time he committed the offense for which he is presently incarcerated.

He describes his use of alcohol as "very light" and does not report illegal drug usage.

Additional Social History: This inmate was originally indicted for the additional offenses of rape and indecent liberties with a child. He claims the charges were dropped when the twelve year old victim's doctor took the witness stand and testified that she had not engaged in intercourse and was a virgin.

A psychiatric evaluation, written in July of 1975, stated that there was no psychiatric contradiction to his working outside the grounds and that there was little likelihood of his attempting to escape or committing aggressive behavior.

During the interview, this inmate presented himself as neat and clean, cooperative, polite, and intelligent. He explains that he served one year at a Northern State Penitentiary and further explains that he had "trouble" with members of gangs, i.e., Vice Lords, Peace Stones, and Devil's Disciples. He says he has been in fights with gang members in the past and that he has no use for gang members. However, he does not report having specific enemies at this or any other correctional facility in the state.

He reports receiving a considerable amount of vocational training in the areas of auto mechanics and machine shop operations. Since incarcerated, he relates that he has received over 1,500 hours vocational training in the "sign shop." He tells that he is primarily interested in auto mechanics. According to this inmate, he completed eleven years of school prior to incarceration. He states that he received a GED in 1974. He says he is presently trying to enter college and that he is interested in small business management, e.g., an auto mechanics garage.

He explains that he was married in 1971 and that he presently remains married. He reports that one child resulted from the relationship and that the child presently resides with his wife out-of-state. He says he and his wife correspond regularly and that she visits on occasion.

Case #512

Offense: **Sentence:**

Aggravated Battery   4-10 Yrs.
Deviate Sexual Assault   4-10 Yrs.

(Sentences ordered to run concurrent)

Interviewed: 1976   **Birthdate:** 1947   **Race:** White

Most Recently Admitted to the Correctional Environment: 1973

Criminal History: This inmate plead guilty to the offenses for which he is presently incarcerated. His records reveal the following: One day in November of 1972, this inmate accosted the victim of the offense on a street in a large midwestern city, forced her behind a parked trailer in a parking lot, then forced her to undress and perform an act of fellatio upon him. This inmate then took the victim's umbrella and inserted it in her vagina causing severe internal injuries.

The victim remained in intensive care 16 days. This inmate was arrested in a tavern. He claims he does not know if he committed the offenses because he had been "drinking" for three days prior to the incident.

He reports that he was arrested numerous times for stealing and shoplifting as a juvenile. He received a one month sentence for larceny in 1966, one year probation (first four months in the House of Corrections) for theft in 1967, and one year to one year and one day for burglary in 1968. He also reports that he received a 90 day sentence for the illegal possession of a pistol in 1969. He describes his use of alcohol as "moderate for the most part" and does not report illegal drug usage.

Additional Social History: During the interview, this inmate stated, "I have a better outlook on things now than I did before. I wasn't really together out on the street."

He reports receiving experience in the areas of machine shop and plastic mold machine operations prior to incarceration. Since incarcerated he has worked primarily in the Knit Shop (over two years). He states that he does not presently have a particular occupational interest.

According to this inmate he completed 11 years of school prior to incarceration. He has not acquired a GED since incarcerated, and stated in this regard, "I didn't figure it would do me any good and I needed the money so I stayed on the pay job over at Knit #2."

He does not report ever having been married or fathering children. He tells that he lived in a common-law relationship from 1969 to 1972. He says he has not communicated with her in three and one-half years. He states that he presently writes "pen pals — different women. I had one come to see me for a year, but she stopped coming about three months ago."

He states that he is not interested in group counseling, commenting, "I don't see where it would do me any good. The only thing I'm interested in is getting out." When questioned regarding release plans, he stated, "get a job of some kind and find me some woman that wants to settle down, that's what I really want."

Case #513

Offense: **Sentence:**

Sexually Dangerous Person   Until Recovery

Interviewed: 1974   **Birthdate:** 1946   **Race:** White

Most Recently Admitted to the Correctional Environment: 1963

Criminal History: His records reveal that in 1963, the County Grand Jury returned an indictment charging him (then age 17) with the crime of rape. Later that year a jury of twelve persons found him to be a "Sexually Dangerous Person."

The Circuit Judge and State's Attorney, described the facts surrounding this case as follows: In 1963, this inmate called the State Employment Bureau in Centerville, and stated that he was a representative of a modeling company. Without verifying the call, the Employment Bureau asked an 18 year old female if she would care to take said employment. The young woman proceeded to a pavilion in a local park where she had been insructed to meet the modeling representative, and met this inmate. He escorted the young woman in her automobile to a rural area and proceeded to make advances toward her. When she resisted, he placed his hands on her throat and began to choke her. After a prolonged period of strangulation, he performed an act of intercourse with the young woman against her will. This inmate later stated to detectives that he had seriously considered killing the young woman to prevent identification.

At the hearing on the petition to have him declared Sexually Dangerous, evidence was presented regarding two other crimes which he had committed in 1961. An 11 year old girl (she was age 8 or 9 when the offense occurred) testified that in 1961, this inmate disrobed her, struck her several times hard enough to cause considerable pain and bruises lasting several days, and then placed his finger into her vagina and otherwise

144

committed lewd and indecent acts upon her person. She further testified that he placed one hand on her mouth and the other on her throat, which caused a temporary strangulation, which ceased before she lost consciousness. She also testified that when she tried to escape, he told her that if she tried to run again, he would tie her, gag her, and throw her in the river and she would drown.

Similarly, a 15 year old girl (she was age 12 or 13 when the offense occurred) testified that in 1961, this inmate threatened her with a butcher knife, forced her to disrobe, and then performed an act of sexual intercourse with her against her will. When she attempted to flee, he reportedly told her that he was going to cut off her arms and legs and cut her body to pieces and that he was going to bury the pieces so that no one could find her.

His records indicate a history of State Mental Hospital placement following sexual assaults prior to 1963. In fact his history caused one psychiatrist to write in 1963, "He was in Centerville State Hospital for treatment and is now in trouble again for the same type of offense." His records indicate that he was incarcerated in the Psychiatric Division at Mid-State from 1964 to 1968.

Additional Social History: During the interview, he presented himself as extremely pessimistic and depressed. He stated "I've been here twelve long nauseating years. I realize I'm never going to get out of this place. I've requested, I've begged; everything short of 'stool pigeon'." During our discussion, he was extremely candid and forceful. He referred to his mother as "that woman" and indicated a great deal of dislike for her. He asserts that he no longer has any real feelings of like or dislike for his mother. He appears to reflect a self-image of isolation and despair. He seems to believe that no one really cares if he lives or dies.

In discussion, he stated, "I know I have a lousy record inside and out." He further states, "The only thing I have not been caught doing is fighting and fucking." He tells that he has been involved in "only" four fights in twelve years. He further states "granted, I've had a couple of kids." In this regard, he states, "I really don't threaten or anything — but I front for

145

them, that's what we call it, I stick up for him." He indicates that he has straightened out some "difficulties" in the past between a kid and a gang.

He reports that he can operate a bulldozer and has had heavy equipment training, some electronics training, home wiring training, and a great deal of experience in the areas of painting (interior and exterior), upholstery, landscaping, gardening, and sewing machine operation. He states that he received a certificate from Remington Rand in office machine repair in 1973 or 1974.

This inmate states that he completed eight years of school prior to incarceration. He reports completing a GED at Mid-State Penitentiary approximately six years ago. He says he "took" three college courses and received a "B" in art appreciation and failed to complete the other two.

He explains that he never married. He says he is not sure that the woman referred to as his mother is his mother or if the person designated as his father is really his father. He states that he has only seen his "father" on one occasion and has no idea where he (his father) presently resides.

When questioned regarding release plans, he stated, "If I was released today, I'd have a job tomorrow." He further comments "It would take me awhile to adjust but I would make it."

Case #514
Offense: **Sentence:**

Burglary   2-6 Yrs.

Interviewed: 1976   **Birthdate:** 1941   **Race:** Black

Most Recently Admitted to the Correctional Environment: 1974

Criminal History: This inmate plead guilty to the offense for which he is presently incarcerated. His records reveal the following: One day in October of 1972, this inmate was discovered inside a grocery store after business hours.

This inmate received a parole to a "halfway house" on April 8, 1974. He violated the Parole Board's order to participate in an alcohol abuse program, as evidenced by his arrest on April 24, 1974, on the charge of public drinking for which he paid a fine of $25. His parole was violated in August of 1974 after his arrest for contributing to the sexual delinquency of a child. His records indicate that he met a twelve year old white girl on a main street in a large urban area one night in July of 1974. After several hours, he took her to his room at the "halfway house" Community Center and had intercourse with her. According to this inmate's statement they had sexual intercourse twice. According to the 12 year old girl they had intercourse three times. The state's attorney reports that the 12 year old and this inmate lived together at this inmate's residence for approximately ten days. During this time the 12 year old girl was listed as a runaway by her parents. The author of the parole violation report stated that there was room for doubt as to the 12 year old girl's willingness to stay with this inmate. However, this inmate plead guilty to contributing to the sexual delinquency of a minor and received an 8 month sentence in November of 1974. This inmate, of course, completed serving the 8 month sentence for contributing to the sexual delinquency of a minor in 1975.

During the interview, this inmate stated that he had been in prison on one other occasion but he could not remember what he was incarcerated for. His records reveal an extremely long and sordid arrest and conviction record. He received a jail sentence for grand larceny in 1959; two years for theft in 1959 (in Virginia); two years for burglary and grand larceny in 1960 (in Alabama); 18 months for grand larceny (auto) in 1963 (in Alabama); and 1-2 years for burglary in 1971 (Illinois). He received parole in January of 1972 after serving approximately 8 months of his 1-2 year sentence and was arrested less than 9 months later for the offense of burglary, for which he is presently incarcerated. His most recent parole, subsequent parole violation, and 8 month sentence for contributing to the sexual delinquency of a minor has, of course, been described above. When questioned regarding his use of alcohol, he stated, "I drank a lot. I drank beer a lot but whiskey most." He does not report using illegal drugs.

Additional Social History: The previously mentioned parole violation report relates that this inmate is illiterate, appears immature and unable to cope with women his own age, and is slightly lazy. His employment record while on parole, according to his parole officer, was as follows: He worked for a foundry in Middletown for a time. However, he was terminated allegedly because he had been caught asleep on the job and had a high tardiness and absenteeism record. He was subsequently employed by a second foundry but his employment only lasted a couple of weeks. The employer reported that he (this inmate) had been caught asleep on the job while standing up and leaning on a broom. The employer indicated that he was worried that this inmate might go to sleep and fall into some machinery in the plant. The employer further indicated that he (this inmate) lied on his application. Apparently this inmate cut his arm just a couple of days after he was employed. This made the employer suspicious and he checked with some of this inmate's previous employers. He learned from one that he (this inmate) had been injured with similar cuts on his arms at his previous employment and had received Workman's Compensation for the injury. Apparently this inmate had put on his application that he had never received Workman's Compensation benefits.

His records also indicate that while on parole, he would frequently go into a small restaurant and stare at the waitresses to the point where they became very uncomfortable and voiced their discomfort to their employer.

He does not report having specific enemies at this or any other correctional facility in the state. However, he says he does have enemies at Mid-State. He says he has only had one fight since his arrival at Mid-State, but complains that gang members have "bothered" him.

Prior to incarceration, he explains that he worked as a cook, a janitor, and waxed cars on occasion. He does not report receiving any vocational training since incarcerated. He relates that he was involved in vocational counseling for approximately two months in 1975. He indicates that he is primarily interested in cooking and electronics.

148

According to this inmate, he completed five years of school prior to incarceration. He comments that he is presently attending school but says he has never acquired an 8th grade diploma.

He reports that he was married in 1968 and divorced in 1969. He tells that he formed a common-law relationship with a woman in 1969 and presently refers to her as his wife. He says he wrote her a letter approximately two months ago but he has not received a letter in return. He does not report ever fathering children.

When questioned regarding release plans, he stated, "I really don't know, but I want to stay out of these places as long as I can."

Case #515

Offense: **Sentence:**

Robbery and Aggravated Battery   3⅓-5 Yrs.

Interviewed: 1976   **Birthdate:** 1940   **Race:** Black

Most Recently Admitted to the Correctional Environment: 1973

Criminal History: This inmate plead not guilty to the offense for which he is presently incarcerated. He was convicted in a bench trial and received a sentence of five to ten years for the offense of robbery and aggravated battery in June of 1973. In August of 1975, an amended mittimus was issued in which this inmate received a sentence reduction to three and one-third to five years for the offense of robbery and aggravated battery. Offense reports indicate that he attacked a sixty year old woman, knocked her to the sidewalk, "and then bumped her head several times on the sidewalk." When the victim began to scream, this inmate reportedly took her black pocketbook and fled. Offense reports also reveal that eight to ten concerned citizens who witnessed the attack surrounded and held this inmate until police officers arrived.

He explains that he was first arrested at age sixteen for shoplifting. He received a sentence of three to ten years for armed robbery in 1958, violated parole in 1964, was returned to prison, and was discharged due to the expiration of his sentence in 1965. He later received a sentence of two years imprisonment in the state of Nebraska for carrying a concealed weapon. His records further reveal that he was arrested for loitering and resisting arrest in 1970 (no disposition shown). He explains that he assaulted a woman. He also received thirty days in jail, in an adjacent state for marijuana possession in 1972. He describes his use of alcohol as "light" and does not report illegal drug usage other than marijuana.

Additional Social History: During the interview, this inmate stated, "I'm one of those fellows that likes to have a good time, but if something interferes with it, I can be dangerous." He has received numerous disciplinary tickets in the past for such offenses as fighting, assault, disregarding orders, insubordination, creating a disturbance, and improper conduct and speech. His records also reveal that he assaulted and fought with numerous police officers in the County Jail as recently as August of 1975. He asserts that his disciplinary tickets are because officers underestimate his intelligence. He further commented, "When you underestimate my intelligence, I get hostile."

He does not report having specific enemies at this or any other correctional facility in the state. However, he states that he does have enemies, but refuses to give names or any specific details. He further indicates that he is not having difficulties adjusting to the correctional environment at the present time.

He insists that he did not possess any vocational training or skills prior to incarceration and asserts that he has not received any vocational training since incarcerated. When questioned regarding his occupational interests, he stated, "Womens is the only thing I'm interested in."

He reports completing eight years of school prior to incarceration. He says he attended school when he was incarcerated in 1958 for armed robbery, but comments that he has not acquired a GED, nor has he been involved in any educational programs in the past fifteen years.

He does not report ever having been married or fathering children. He explains that he corresponds regularly with his mother and father who presently reside in an adjacent state and that they visit him on occasion.

When questioned regarding his release plans, he stated, "I'm goin' on back to my mother and father's crib I hope, and try to do the right thing, try not to get too excited again messing with prostitutes, ya know, or stickin up somebody."

Case #516

Offense: **Sentence:**

Armed Robbery   5-10 Yrs.

Interviewed: 1976   **Birthdate:** 1940   **Race:** White

Most Recently Admitted to the Correctional Environment: 1972

Criminal History: This inmate plead guilty to the offense for which he is presently incarcerated. He explains that he and an accomplice robbed a service station while armed with an empty shotgun. He says he was under the influence of prescription drugs at the time and had been drinking vodka. He asserts that he did not "come to his senses" until "about three days later." He reports receiving one year probation in 1958 for auto theft. He received a one year prison sentence in 1958 after violating probation. He states that he attempted to escape from a minimum security institution in 1959, and "tied up an officer" in the process. As a result, he indicates that he received a sentence of one and one-half to three years for kidnapping in 1959. He was paroled in 1961, and explains that he violated parole in 1961, was returned to prison, and again released in 1962. He was arrested for forgery in late 1962 and received a one to two year sentence. He was again paroled in 1964. He was arrested in 1965 and received a ten year sentence for armed robbery. He states that he was released again in 1971 and received his present sentence in 1972.

He describes his use of alcohol as "moderate" and states that he has experimented with illegal drugs in the past. His records indicate that he has had an "alcohol problem" for numerous years.

Additional Social History: During the interview, he explained that his past criminal behavior was the result of economic deprivation. He commented, "I never had nothing to look forward to; I couldn't even buy a new shirt." Regarding interpersonal relations, he stated, "I don't associate with everybody. I have two or three friends and that's it. I was the same way on the outside."

He reports that he has spent approximately fourteen years incarcerated to date and indicates that he is tired of serving time. During the interview, he was polite and cooperative and he seized every opportunity to assert that he will never again commit a crime.

He reports that he did "farm work" prior to incarceration. Since incarcerated, he relates that he has received training in the area of meat cutting and processing, and dental technology. He states that he received a certificate for 1,500 hours of training in the area of meat cutting and processing in 1973 and received a certificate in dental technology in 1974. He says he is primarily interested in dental technology.

According to this inmate, he completed ten years of school prior to incarceration. He has never acquired a GED.

He explains that although he has never married, he did form a common-law relationship with a woman during the years 1961 and 1962. He states that children did not result from the relationship. He reports that his mother lives in-state and that they correspond regularly. He comments that he also corresponds regularly with his "girlfriend", and asserts that she "has been with me since 1972 and has helped me a great deal."

When released he plans to marry his "girlfriend" and work for an oil company.

Case #517

Offense: **Sentence:**

Aggravated Kidnapping 100-150 Yrs.
Rape 100-150 Yrs.
Theft 5-10 Yrs.

(The above sentences were ordered to run concurrent)

Attempted Murder 10-15 Yrs.

(Consecutive to the sentences above)

Interviewed: 1976 **Birthdate:** 1940 **Race:** White

Most Recently Admitted to the Correctional Environment: 1969

Criminal History: This inmate plead not guilty to the offenses for which he is presently incarcerated. He was convicted by a jury verdict. He was sentenced to serve his two sentences of 100-150 years for aggravated kidnapping and rape concurrently with the 5-10 year sentence for theft. The 10-15 year sentence for attempted murder was ordered to run consecutive. His records reveal the following: one day in October of 1968, (in an adjacent state) the victim (a young married woman) left work at approximately 11:45 p.m. and met with eight other female employees of the telephone company, where she was employed, as they had agreed earlier. They met in a restaurant and lounge. Shortly thereafter, this inmate and his friend (accomplice) joined the party of women. Casual conversation ensued and this inmate let it be known that he and his friend (accomplice) were traveling west, and he asked various women for a ride. At approximately two o'clock when the group broke up, the victim reluctantly agreed to drive the two men in a westerly direction toward her home.

During the course of the ride, this inmate produced a

153

weapon (believed to be a .22 caliber automatic pistol) and informed the victim that he and his accomplice intended to rape her. Shortly thereafter, they turned off the highway and this inmate's accomplice raped the woman while he (this inmate) held a gun to her head. Both men then rejected the victim's pleas to release her and indicated to her that they had to take her with them to avoid capture by the police, because they had recently been released from a nearby penitentiary. This inmate then "commandeered" the victim's automobile, and proceeded to drive West. Many miles later the car was again driven off the highway and parked on a deserted road where this inmate and his accomplice physically assaulted and struck the woman until she again submitted to an act of intercourse with this inmate's accomplice and then involuntarily submitted to an act of intercourse with this inmate. Then, all three entered the vehicle and continued in a westerly direction. At various points along the approximately 300 mile journey this inmate and his accomplice looted the victim's purse and when she attempted to resist their demands for money, she was struck and slapped in the face and body. After entering the state where Mid-State Penitentiary is located, this inmate drove the victim's car to a deserted farm road. At this point, the victim again pleaded to be released but this inmate indicated that they had to make sure that she would never identify them because they would never be taken alive and did not want to go back to the penitentiary. Then this inmate held a gun to the victim's head, and his accomplice again forcibly raped her. Then while his accomplice held a knife on her, this inmate forcibly raped her. After having intercourse with the victim, this inmate attempted to strangle her in the back seat of her automobile. However, she resisted and was subsequently dragged from her car by the two men where she was kicked in the face and head. This inmate then held the victim's hands behind her back, forced her to bend over, and placed the .22 caliber revolver in the back of her head, and then shot her four times; once in the back of the head, once through the right eye, once through the neck, and once through the right hand. She was thereby rendered unconscious. Thinking her dead, this inmate and his accomplice proceeded to cover her with straw and manure. They took her personal belongings and left in her automobile.

154

Approximately one hour later, the victim regained consciousness and made her way approximately ¾ of a mile back to an expressway where she was observed by a passing motorist. The motorist observed her staggering across an open field and observed that she was "covered with blood," was "bleeding profusely from the head and neck," had "two black eyes," and "various bruises and lacerations from her face and body." She was taken to a nearby Community Hospital where her pulse was determined to be 70/0 at the time of admittance and she was found to have lost approximately five pints of blood. X-rays and examinations by surgeons indicated that both bullets that entered her head were still lodged in her head. One of the bullets was lodged in her brain and there were approximately 24 bullet fragments scattered throughout her head and brain area. She was in critical condition for approximately two weeks. Her right hand was broken from the bullet wound and her vision was originally impaired as a result of the bullet wound to the eye. The bullet wound to the neck severed the muscle tissues surrounding the spinal column and it was necessary to transplant a bone from her right leg and fuse it to the spinal column in order to support her head. Doctors have indicated that as a result of the injuries she sustained from the four bullet wounds, she will be permanently disfigured and disabled. At the time of the incident the victim was 31 years of age, married, and the mother of three children.

This inmate and his accomplice were initially incarcerated in a city jail. They attempted to escape from jail at the time of a scheduled preliminary hearing by tearing out the ceiling in their cell. Subsequently, they were transferred to the county where they again attempted an escape by attempting to kick out an exit window.

He explains that he was first arrested at age 13 in 1953, for auto theft. He reports that he was subsequently sent to a foster home for one year. He was arrested in August of 1956 for auto theft, for which, according to this inmate, he received three years probation. He was arrested by military authorities in 1959, because, as he tells it, he was absent without leave which resulted in his receiving an undesirable discharge in January of 1960.

This inmate states that he received a sentence of 1-14 years for second degree burglary in California in October of 1961. He was arrested for breaking and entering in the nighttime in December of 1961 in the state of Michigan. He received a sentence of 2½-15 years for the offense of breaking and entering in the nighttime in January of 1962. He was paroled to Illinois from Michigan in March of 1964. He was arrested for breaking and entering in the nighttime in May of 1964 and again in July of 1964. He relates that he was returned to a Michigan penitentiary in March of 1965 for violating parole. He states that he was again paroled in September of 1966 and was arrested for assault with a deadly weapon in December of the same year. His records indicate that he was found not guilty by a jury trial of assault with a deadly weapon. Thus, he was continued on parole. It is not known whether he was still on parole when arrested for the present offenses. He describes his use of alcohol as moderate and does not report illegal drug usage.

Additional Social History: His social history reveals that he is the product of his mother's second marriage; that he was two when his parents were divorced; and that there have been a number of subsequent marriages by each of his parents. He estimates that his mother has been married approximately seven times.

He was expelled from school on several occasions before finally dropping out at the age of 15. He enlisted in the Army in 1958. However, several months later he was placed in the stockade for a lengthy period because of repeated A.W.O.L.'s and escapes. The Psychiatric Report written by an Army Psychiatrist when this inmate was 19, speaks of him as untrustworthy, anti-authoritarian, "not worth the time and effort required to rehabilitate him." The report also mentions violent, meaningless outbursts, and the fact that this inmate, at that time, had little regard for the rights of others. He was considered to be free of mental illness, but an antisocial personality. The psychiatric report also commented, "this inmate is not in need of mental treatment and not mentally retarded."

During the interview, this inmate stated:

I'd say I'm not a very good person sometimes. I try to be. I try to help other people. I get upset easy, easier than most people. Small things irritate me.

Since incarcerated this inmate has assaulted guards by striking them, and on one occasion he threw a club made from a stool leg at a guard. He has been apprehended in possession of numerous weapons, e.g., clubs, shields, and knives. It is noted that he also sexually assaulted and beat his cell partner. He has had good time revoked on both maximum and minimum sentences.

He does not report having specific enemies at this or any other correctional facility in the state. He further indicates that he is not having unusual difficulties adjusting to the correctional environment at the present time. However, he complains that he has difficulties adjusting to cell partners, both in the past and at the present time. He has requested a private cell.

He reports receiving "a little baking experience" prior to incarceration. Since incarcerated, he reports receiving a little training in sign painting, although he says he is primarily interested in art, i.e., water colors on paper.

According to this inmate, he completed ten years of school prior to incarceration. He indicates that he has never pursued a GED. He also comments that he is not interested in a GED.

This inmate explains that he was married in 1967, and divorced in 1969. He tells that his wife was 17 years old when he married her and that one child resulted from the union, born in 1968.

He explains that he is presently a member of the "Prisoners' Rights Organization for the Liquidation and Arbitration of Wrongs, Inc." He says he would like to open an art gallery when released.

Case #518

Offense: **Sentence:**

Voluntary Manslaughter   7-14 Yrs.

Interviewed: 1976   **Birthdate:** 1939   **Race:** White

Most Recently Admitted to the Correctional Environment: 1972

Criminal History: This inmate pled guilty to the offense for which he is presently incarcerated. In November of 1970, at 1:30 a.m. at a tavern populated by American Indians, the victim (a female) and this inmate had an argument. Both were drinking heavily and the victim, although married, was having an affair with this inmate. This inmate slashed the victim's neck with a knife and fled the tavern. He explains that he cut his girlfriend's throat in a bar, although he asserts he just intended to frighten her.

He was first arrested at age 15 for arson after burning down a neighbor's home in accordance with his grandfather's instructions. He received a 25 year sentence for robbery with aggravation in 1958. This inmate explains that he and a friend wrestled with and robbed a hotel manager.

He received parole in 1963 from an Iowa correctional facility. He was arrested in 1964 in Indiana and received a one year sentence for petty larceny. He reports that he escaped from an Indiana State Farm in 1964 and was not apprehended until 1966. His records reveal that he received a sentence of 1-5 years for escape from an Indiana correctional facility in 1966. He states that he served approximately 19 months in Indiana correctional facilities before being paroled in 1968. He describes his use of alcohol as "social" and does not report illegal drug usage.

Additional Social History: During our discussion, he stated, "I know when I go out of here I'm going to go out bitter, but not

158

bitter enough that I'll break any laws." During the interview, he expressed a great deal of remorse about "cutting his girlfriend's throat."

He reports working as a welder and machine operator prior to incarceration. He claims he can do any type of work. He relates that he has received three years training as a locksmith since incarcerated. He states that he is primarily interested in "outside work."

According to this inmate, he completed six years of school prior to incarceration. He says he attended school for 19 months while incarcerated in Indiana correctional facilities.

According to his records, his parents were separated when he was about four years old. His mother died of cancer several years ago. His father was a painter by trade and owned a whiskey store. His father drank and failed to support his family. He (this inmate's father) died one month after the death of his wife (this inmate's mother). This inmate then stayed with his aunt. His brother is in a penitentiary for shooting a man. This inmate reports that he has never married or fathered children. He says he corresponds regularly with his sister who resides in-state and a niece who resides in an adjacent state.

Case #519

Offense: **Sentence:**

Rape   30-60 Yrs.
Rape   40-75 Yrs.

(Sentences ordered to run consecutive)

Interviewed: 1976   **Birthdate:** 1936   **Race:** Black

Most Recently Admitted to the Correctional Environment: 1964

Criminal History: This inmate plead not guilty to the offenses for which he is presently incarcerated. He was convicted by a jury verdict and in July of 1973, received a sentence of 40-75 years for rape to be served consecutively to his prior sentence of 30-60 years for rape which was imposed in 1964. The Official Statement of Facts regarding his most recent rape conviction reveals the following: One day in December of 1972 while this inmate was incarcerated in the minimum security unit of a Northern State Penitentiary, he unlawfully entered the residence of the Warden's Assistant at approximately 2:30 p.m. He then raped and stabbed the Warden's Assistant's 16 year old daughter with a screw driver. This attack occurred at the Warden's Assistant's residence which was located just west of the minimum security unit. The attack lasted approximately 15 minutes, and this inmate left the home apparently thinking that the victim was dead. When friends of the victim arrived at the house, they took her immediately to her father at the prison. She reported that this inmate had raped her and tried to kill her. This inmate was indicted for attempted murder, in that it was alleged that he attempted to kill his rape victim in 1972. However, the jury found him not guilty of attempted murder.

This inmate's records further reveal that he was convicted by a jury verdict of raping a 20 year old woman in the laundry room of an apartment building after abducting her from the apartment elevator. The offense reportedly occurred in December of 1963, and he received a sentence of 30-60 years in July of 1964.

This inmate's records indicate that he received a sentence of 1-5 years for larceny in Tennessee in 1955. He received parole in April of 1957, and violated parole in December of 1957. He states that he was finally released from Tennessee correctional facilities in 1959 at the expiration of his sentence. He was arrested on numerous occasions between the years of 1962 and 1964, for offenses such as: tampering with auto, criminal damage to property (30 day sentence), investigation of receiving stolen property, contributing to delinquency, investigation of rape, and investigation of rape on charge of indecent liberties.

This inmate received a 5-10 year sentence for robbery in 1964, in that he robbed his rape victim in 1963. The 5-10 year

160

sentence was served concurrently with his 30-60 year sentence and has been discharged. He describes his use of alcohol as "social" and does not report illegal drug usage.

Additional Social History: During our discussion, this inmate described himself stating, "I likes to treat a person as I want to be treated. I don't treat people different because of their color. I dislike this racist thing, I like to see people love each other."

He reports that an inmate here at Mid-State has been telling other inmates what he did while incarcerated at the Northern Prison and the reason for his transfer. He states that he would like to be kept separated from this inmate.

He reports receiving experience as an auto mechanic, brick-layer, and farm laborer prior to incarceration. He explains that since incarcerated he has received two training certificates, one in art in 1968, and the other in sewing machine repair in 1969.

According to this inmate, he completed seven years of school prior to incarceration. He states that he has not received an 8th grade diploma since incarcerated. However, he asserts that he has taken Bible courses in the past and is presently taking Bible courses.

He does not report ever having been married or fathering children. He tells that he corresponds with his parents in-state.

When questioned regarding release plans, this inmate related that he planned "to go into some kind of business for myself — art or interior decorating."

Case #520

Offense: **Sentence:**

Armed Robbery   75-100 Yrs.
Attempted Rape   13-14 Yrs.

Attempted Rape   10-14 Yrs.
Rape   4 Yrs. to 4 Yrs. and 1 Day

(All sentences have been aggregated to 98-128 years)

Interviewed: 1976   **Birthdate:** 1934   **Race:** Black

Most Recently Admitted to the Correctional Environment: 1970

Criminal History: This inmate plead not guilty to armed robbery and the two counts of attempted rape, but he did plead guilty to the charge of rape. The above sentences have been aggregated to a sentence of ninety-eight to one hundred and twenty-eight years. The Official Statement of Facts regarding the armed robbery and one attempted rape describes the offense as follows: The victim saw this inmate get out of a white Cadillac convertible and follow her into the building. As she started up a stairway to a second floor apartment, this inmate grabbed her and pulled her down the stairs. He then threatened to kill her if she attempted to scream. He put a knife to her throat and began to fondle her and remove her clothing. He also attempted to kiss her. She kept talking to him, trying to convince him to leave her alone. This attack continued for five to ten minutes. He finally made her completely disrobe and sit on the steps. Then he removed $7.00 from her purse and put it in his pocket. Next, he reached down and attempted to push her down on her back. His penis was exposed and he attempted to place it into her. However, before he could accomplish this, he reached orgasm and ejaculated on her leg. He then ran from the hallway.

The Official Statement of Facts regarding the attempted rape for which he received a sentence of thirteen to fourteen years reveals that he grabbed an eighteen year old woman in a stairwell and at knifepoint, kissed her, threw her into a corner, pulled her dress up and panties down, exposed himself, and tried to penetrate her. However, before he was able to do so he reached orgasm and ejaculated on the outside of the victim's body and clothing.

Regarding the offense of rape for which he received a sentence of four years to four years and one day, the Official

162

Statement of Facts reveals the following: One September day in 1968, at 6:25 p.m., the victim was walking down the hallway of the third floor of a Y.M.C.A. building. This inmate approached the victim and engaged her in conversation. He then produced a knife, forced her into the stairway of the third floor, and raped her. He was arrested for the above offenses in October of 1968.

He received a four to ten year sentence for assault to rape in 1953 and a sentence of fifty years for rape in 1957. He was classified as a Sexually Dangerous Person at the institutional level, i.e., in the prison environment. However, in September 1959, this inmate was reclassified for a Northern State Maximum Security Prison from the Psychiatric Division at Mid-State Penitentiary as no longer sexually dangerous at the institutional level. It was noted at that time that due to the length of sentence and background of aggressiveness, this man was more adequately segregated at the Northern Prison. In November of 1959, this inmate was returned from the Northern Prison to the Mid-State Psychiatric Division as a sexually dangerous person. The Re-Classification Report noted that this inmate was returned to the Mid-State Psychiatric Division following official apprehension in a sexually abnormal act.

Interestingly, this inmate was on parole after serving ten years of a fifty year sentence for rape (received in 1957) when he committed the offenses for which he is presently incarcerated.

When questioned regarding his use of alcohol prior to incarceration, he commented that he had a tendency to get drunk to avoid responsibilities. When questioned regarding the frequency with which he became intoxicated, he stated, "A good one about every month." He further stated that he used microdot acid and "downers" prior to incarceration.

Additional Social History: This inmate asserts that if he is not drunk, he is alright, but when he gets "high," he tends to lose control and wants to rape women that appeal to him. He says he has a real difficulty in controlling sexual urges when he's "high." During the interview, he stated, "When I do get high, I do crazy things. That's the lack of not knowing yourself, feeling inferior like you can't get out and get a girl."

Although this inmate has a lengthy history of alcohol abuse, he insists that he has "given it up." He claims that he could drink alcohol while incarcerated if he so desired, but he "gave it up." He states that if he can handle incarceration without alcohol as a crutch, he can handle the community outside the correctional environment.

His records indicate that he has a tendency to talk a great deal in an effort to persuade staff members that he has learned his lesson, and that he will never touch another drop of alcohol.

He does not report having enemies at this or any other correctional facility in the state. He further indicates that he is not having difficulties in adjusting to the correctional environment at the present time.

This inmate states that he is a heavy equipment operator and he reports receiving seventeen certificates in heavy equipment operation and related fields (diesel and gas mechanics) since incarcerated in 1968.

According to this inmate, he completed nine years of school prior to incarceration. He reports completing a GED in 1962 or 1963 at Mid-State Penitentiary. He indicates that he is not interested in the college program.

He states that he was married in 1957. He explains that three children resulted from the marriage. He says his daughter presently attends college out-of-state and that his two sons reside with his wife who teaches special education out-of-state. He indicates that he corresponds with his family and that they visit him regularly.

He says he plans to return to his wife and children and pursue an occupation in heavy equipment operation when released.

Case #521

Offense: **Sentence:**

Robbery   4 Yrs. to 4 Yrs. and 1 Day
Murder   75-150 Yrs.

(Sentences ordered to run concurrent)

Interviewed: 1976   **Birthdate:** 1934   **Race:** Black

Most Recently Admitted to the Correctional Environment: 1972

Criminal History: This inmate plead guilty to robbery and not
guilty to murder. At this point in time, the above sentence for
robbery has been discharged. He has a long and sordid history
of criminal offenses dating back to 1952. He received 30 days
in jail for tampering with an automobile in 1952; two 2-8 and
one 1-20 year sentence for robbery in 1959; and one 2-3 year
sentence and one 3-4 year sentence for two counts of robbery in
1968. His records indicate that he has violated probation and
parole with awesome regularity and the last time paroled, he
only remained in the free community approximately five weeks
before he was arrested for the robbery which resulted in a 4
year to 4 year and 1 day sentence.
     While incarcerated in a Northern Maximum Security Peni-
tentiary in 1973, this inmate murdered a guard (correctional officer). The Statement of Facts reveals the following: One day in
1973, two correctional officers were letting unassigned inmates
out of their cells. At that time, this inmate approached the officers and asked them if he could get a painting out of a cell.
Both officers told this inmate no because they were busy handling the transfer of inmates. A few minutes later, this inmate
approached one of the officers, pulled out of a knife and began
stabbing him. After stabbing the officer several times, this inmate kicked him under the railing causing him to fall approx-

imately 25 feet to the floor below. The pathologist who testified at the trial stated that the officer was stabbed eight times, and that his death was due to a stab wound which pierced the heart.

When questioned regarding his use of alcohol prior to incarceration, this inmate indicated that he "has trouble when he drinks" and stated, "I can't drink." He does not report using illegal drugs.

Additional Social History: During the interview, he commented, "I try to read and write and go to school. As a whole, I'm trying to find myself — just find out where I'm at." It appears that this inmate has spent approximately 15 of the last 17 years in various "correctional centers." He has a history of violence and has been arrested for rape and aggravated battery in the past. During his last robbery he threatened to kill the victim (a woman), threw her against a building, and then threw her down on the sidewalk.

He denies having any specific enemies at this or any other correctional facility in the state, but explains that other inmates threatened his life at the correctional center in 1973. He further indicates that he is not having difficulties adjusting to the correctional environment at the present time.

He explains that he worked as a manual laborer, construction worker, and truck driver prior to incarceration. Since incarcerated, he says he has received "a little" training in the areas of welding and painting. He reports that he is primarily interested in acquiring a GED. He says he only completed seven years of school prior to incarceration.

He relates that he has never married, although he has fathered two children, one in-state and one in California. He says his mother died in 1939 or 1940 and that his father presently resides in Tennessee. He reports that he only corresponds with a couple of friends and a cousin.

166

Case #522

Offense: **Sentence:**

Murder   99 Yrs.

Interviewed: 1976   **Birthdate:** 1931   **Race:** White

Most Recently Admitted to the Correctional Environment: 1958

Criminal History: He was received at the Northern Classification Unit in 1958, and was transferred to Mid-State Penitentiary in 1959. He has remained at Mid-State since that time. He plead guilty to the offense for which he is presently incarcerated. He admits to killing a saleslady in a clothing store who resisted his sexual advances. The murder was a rather brutal one in which the victim's throat was slashed repeatedly with a knife. A statement by the State's Attorney indicates that after the murder conviction, he admitted strangling and killing his 12 year old sister 12 years prior to his arrest for the present offense, at which time this inmate was 15 years old.

The State's Attorney also reported that this inmate had been arrested in 1947, as a juvenile delinquent, for shooting out a neighbor's window. The shooting was apparently retaliatory because the neighbor woman had asked him not to come on her property. He describes his use of alcohol as "moderate" and denies illegal drug usage.

Additional Social History: Since incarcerated, this inmate has received very few disciplinary citations. His records indicate that he has not been cited for a disciplinary infraction since 1967. However, it is noted in his file that he recently had some interpersonal difficulties with a female counselor, while in minimum security, which resulted in his return to the general prison population for a period of time.

He denies having enemies at Mid-State or any other correctional facility in the state. During the interview, he stated, "I

167

get along all right with everybody."

He tells that he has worked in the Upholstery Shop at Mid-State for the past five years. He further states that he had previously worked in the Knit Shop at Mid-State for approximately 11 years.

He reports completing seven years of school. He asserts that he started a GED program in March or April of last year but did not finish it. The State's Attorney's statement regarding this inmate's education reveals the following: His school history indicates he was stubborn and at times mean to other children. He did not mingle freely with other children. He was slow in school, and was finally withdrawn from school by his parents when he reached the age of sixteen.

He explains that his mother is no longer living and that he corresponds with his father who presently resides in-state. He states that he has never been married.

When questioned regarding his release plans, he stated, "I'm very much interested in upholstery work and if I'm released, I'll take up upholstery work on the streets."

During the interview, he appeared older than his years and extremely slow-witted. It also appears that he lacks verbal skills which would facilitate meaningful interpersonal relations.

Case #523

Offense: **Sentence:**

Rape 25-50 Yrs.
Armed Robbery 15-30 Yrs.

(Sentences ordered to run concurrent)

Interviewed: 1976   **Birthdate:** 1931   **Race:** White

Most Recently Admitted to the Correctional Environment: 1965

Criminal History: This inmate was initially convicted of Aggravated Kidnapping and received a sentence of twenty to forty years along with the two above-mentioned offenses. His records reveal that an amended mittimus was received deleting the sentence and conviction on aggravated kidnapping. The statement of the Circuit Judge and State's Attorney indicates that this inmate along with three male accomplices robbed a man and his female companion while armed with pistols. It is further reported that the woman was abducted and transported to an area a few miles away where she was raped by this inmate and his accomplices. All three of this inmate's accomplices plead guilty to rape receiving sentences of two to twenty-five, five to twenty-five, and five to twenty years. The charges of armed robbery and aggravated kidnapping were subsequently dismissed against the three associates.

He describes his use of alcohol as moderate and denies illegal drug usage. He has a history of arrests for larceny, robbery, and burglary. His records indicate that he received a prison sentence of one to ten years for Larceny in 1948 as well as a prison sentence of two to four years for Burglary in 1961.

Additional Social History: During the interview, he stated, "I do my own time. If I see another man doing something, that's up to him." He describes himself as "easy going." During our discussion, he was extremely polite.

His records indicate that he has not received a single disciplinary ticket during his ten years of incarceration.

He explains that prior to incarceration, he worked as a laborer. He tells that while incarcerated, he has received training in the area of heavy equipment operation, which involves on-the-job training, receiving his certificate in heavy equipment operation in 1973 or 1974. He also reports receiving a certificate in diesel mechanics in 1973 or 1974.

He states that he completed seven years of school prior to incarceration. He explains that he is not interested in additional education and says since he has a trade, it is really not necessary.

He tells that he was married in 1951 and divorced in 1953. He says one son resulted from his first marriage. He says he was married a second time in 1959 and divorced in 1967 and that three daughters and one son resulted from the second marriage. He indicates that he corresponds with his children regularly. He reports that his mother and father are deceased.

VI
Young Offenders — Recent Trends

On November 14, 1976, Parade magazine published an article entitled "Has The Time Come To Get Tough With Juvenile Criminals?" President Ford was quoted as saying:

> If they are big enough to commit vicious crimes against society they are big enough to be punished by society. Too many violent and street-wise juveniles are using their age as a cloak of immunity. Detention may not help the juvenile, but it will certainly help his potential victims.

The article pointed out that many states were getting tougher with juveniles by issuing stiffer sentences. The State of New York was cited as an example of the "get tough approach" because New York had just imposed "a two-year minimum and five-year maximum confinement on 14 and 15 year olds found guilty of felonies."

Ironically, on June 30, 1978, an article entitled "Young Killer Sentenced to 18 months" about a 15 year old New York boy appeared in the Austin American-Statesman. The article stated:

> The 15-year-old boy held the gun three inches from the subway rider's left temple, squeezed the trigger, and killed.

Why?

> 'He got a kick out of blowing them away,' said a cousin who was with him when the boy killed Moises Perez, 38, March 28.

> That killing and a history of violence resulted in a jail sentence of only 18 months, handed down Wednesday. He was convicted of juvenile delinquency.

> Nine days before he was sentenced, the boy, armed with a pistol he had bought on the street for $65, shot and killed Noel Perez, 45, during another subway ride. That time he left a sneaker print in a pool of blood.

> Two days after that slaying, the boy, whose name was not released, appeared in Family Court on an unrelated pickpocketing charge during which transit police called him 'extremely dangerous', and recommended he be remanded to a juvenile detention center.

> But the judge, despite a city lawyer's prediction that the boy would commit a more serious crime, released him in custody of his mother.

> Two days later, the boy — and his cousin — were surprised in a trainyard by motorman Anthony Lamorata. The boy shot Lamorata in the back, wounding him seriously.

> 'He's the most violent kid I've ever seen in Family Court,' said one prosecutor. 'He's a cold-blooded killer.'

> Locked up in the Spofford Juvenile Detention Center after a transit police investigation, the boy told another inmate, 'I'll kill you if you sit down next to me.' He stabbed the inmate in the neck with a fork.

> The boy once bragged of having a record of eight

172

robbery arrests which began when he was nine years old.

He had spent seven months in the upstate Brookwood Center for Youth where he intimidated the staff, bludgeoning two members with a hammer. In one day, he reportedly raped another boy, stole a truck, attempted to run over a social worker and menaced the director and 10 staff members with a crow bar.

When a psychiatrist was called, the boy beat him up.

During his Family Court appearances, he spat on an assistant district attorney, hurled a glass ash tray at a guard, cursed at the judge and said he was keeping a list of people he intended to kill when he escaped, including the cook at Spofford and a prison van driver who drove him to court.

Despite his background and the recent two killings and wounding of Lamorata, the boy was sentenced to 18 months to five years — the maximum Family Court Judge Edith Miller could impose under the state's juvenile offenders law.

'They put this kid away for 18 months,' one detective said, 'In 18 months and a day, somebody's going to get killed.'

The FBI *Uniform Crime Reports* (1977:182) reveal that the number of persons under the age of 18 arrested for committing violent crimes (murder, forcible rape, robbery, and aggravated assault) increased from 15,342 in 1960 to 60,352 in 1975 — an increase of 293.4%. In 1976, according to the *Uniform Crime Reports* (1977:183), the number of arrests for the violent offenses listed above increased to 74,715 for those under the age of 18.

Increased violence by young people is also apparent in Junior High Schools and High Schools. According to the National Education Association, more than 60,900 teachers were attacked by students last year (Austin American-Statesman, 12-27-78). Since 1972 classroom murders have increased 18 percent, rapes have increased 40 percent, and assaults have increased 77 percent. Dr. Alfred Bloch, a psychoanalyst who recently concluded a five-year study of battered teachers, found that battered teachers react the same as soldiers who have fought too long on the front lines. They suffer from ailments like migraine headaches, ulcers, hypertension, depression, and insomnia. Bloch asserts, "When the teacher in classroom A is raped or assaulted, think what it does to the teacher in classroom B or C or D. She is living in constant anxiety, always wondering, 'when is it going to be my turn?' "

In addition to the increased number of violent acts committed by young offenders, we find that the majority of those individuals arrested for burglary, breaking or entering, motor vehicle theft, arson, or vandalism in 1976 were also seventeen years of age or younger (*Uniform Crime Reports* 1977:183). However, we also find that of all the juveniles taken into custody by the police in 1976, approximately half were handled within the police department and released without formal charge or referral to any court (*Uniform Crime Reports*, 1977:220).

VII
Recommendations For Prevention

Extensive investigations conducted by the Presidential Commission on Law Enforcement and Administration of Justice (1968:177) reveal that delinquency in slum areas is a disproportionately high percentage of all delinquency and includes a disproportionately high number of dangerous acts. "Instead of turning out men and women who conform to the American norm at least overtly, at least enough to stay out of jail, the slums are producing the highest rates of crime, vice, and financial dependence (President's Commission on Law Enforcement and Administration of Justice, 1968:178)."

The Commission pointed out that "it is with young people that prevention efforts are most needed and hold the greatest promise (1968:175)." With this in mind the Commission made 40 explicit recommendations. They are as follows:

Efforts, both private and public, should be intensified to:

1. Reduce unemployment and devise methods of providing minimum family income.
2. Reexamine and revise welfare regulations so that

they contribute to keeping the family together.
3. Improve housing and recreation facilities.
4. Insure availability of family planning assistance.
5. Provide help in problems of domestic management and child care.
6. Make counseling and therapy easily obtainable.
7. Develop activities that involve the whole family together.
8. Involve young people in community activities.
9. Train and employ youth as subprofessional aides.
10. Establish Youth Services Bureaus to provide and coordinate programs for young people.
11. Increase involvement of religious institutions, private social agencies, fraternal groups, and other community organizations in youth programs.
12. Provide community residential centers.

In order that slum children may receive the best rather than the worst education in the Nation, efforts, both private and public, should be intensified to:
13. Secure financial support for necessary personnel, buildings, and equipment.
14. Improve the quality and quantity of teachers and facilities in the slum school.
15. Combat racial and economic school segregation.

In order that schools may better adapt to the particular educational problems of the slum child, efforts, both private and public, should be intensified to:
16. Help slum children make up for inadequate pre-school preparation.
17. Deal better with behavior problems.
18. Relate instructional material to condition of life in the slums.

In order that schools may better prepare students for the future, efforts, both private and public, should be intensified to:

19. Raise the aspirations and expectations of students capable of higher education.
20. Review and revise present programs for students not going to college.
21. Further develop job placement services in schools.
22. In order that schools may become more responsive to community needs and parental expectations, efforts, both private and public, should be intensified to develop cooperation between schools and their communities.

Efforts, both private and public, should be intensified to:

23. Prepare youth for employment.
24. Provide youth with information about employment opportunities.
25. Reduce barriers to employment posed by discrimination, the misuse of criminal records, and maintenance of rigid job qualifications.
26. Create new employment opportunities.
27. To the greatest feasible extent, police departments should formulate policy guidelines for dealing with juveniles.
28. All officers should be acquainted with the special characteristics of adolescents, particularly those of the social, racial, and other specific groups with which they are likely to come in contact.
29. Custody of a juvenile (both prolonged street stops and stationhouse visits) should be limited to instances where there is objective, specifiable ground for suspicion.
30. Every stop that includes a frisk or an interrogation of more than a few preliminary identifying questions should be recorded in a strictly confidential report.

31. Police forces should make full use of the central diagnosing and coordinating services of the Youth Services Bureau. Station adjustment should be limited to release and referral; it should not include hearings or the imposition of sanctions by the police. Court referral by the police should be restricted to those cases involving serious criminal conduct or repeated misconduct of a more than trivial nature.

32. Communities should establish neighborhood youth-serving agencies — Youth Services Bureaus — located if possible in comprehensive neighborhood community centers and receiving juveniles (delinquent and nondelinquent) referred by the police, the juvenile court, parents, schools, and other sources.

33. Juvenile courts should make fullest feasible use of preliminary conferences to dispose of cases short of adjudication.

34. Juvenile courts should employ consent decrees wherever possible to avoid adjudication while still settling juvenile cases and treating offenders.

35. The movement for narrowing the juvenile court's jurisdiction should be continued.

36. Counsel should be appointed as a matter of course wherever coercive action is a possibility, without requiring any affirmative choice by child or parent.

37. Juvenile court hearings should be divided into an adjudicatory hearing and a dispositional one, and the evidence admissible at the adjudicatory hearing should be so limited that findings are not dependent upon or unduly influenced by hearsay, gossip, rumor, and other unreliable types of information.

38. Notice should be given well in advance of any scheduled court proceedings, including intake, detention, and waiver hearings, and should set forth the alleged misconduct with particularity.

39. Adequate and appropriate separate detention

facilities for juveniles should be provided.
40. Legislation should be enacted restricting both authority to detain and the circumstances under which detention is permitted.

For many years would-be experts have argued that society should subsidize the family and keep the family together in order to alleviate delinquency as well as many other social problems, e.g., unemployment, illiterarcy, etc. The Presidential Commission on Law Enforcement and Administration of Justice reflects this traditional approach as evidenced by their recommendations for providing a minimum family income and revising welfare regulations so that they contribute to keeping the family together.

Contrary to the Commission's recommendations and popular sociological folklore, I have never been comfortable with the idea of supporting parents. Through welfare assistance, we are not only supporting the family economically, we are supporting parental supervision, discipline, and whatever child rearing practices those parents engage in. Through welfare expenditures virtually every state in the Union supports incompetent parents. Parents who do not encourage school attendance, personal hygiene, courtesy, non-violence, respect for property rights, self-sufficiency, etc. It seems as though the only qualifying characteristics needed to be a subsidized mother are as follows:

(1) Poverty.
(2) Functioning female organs, capable of producing a baby or babies.
(3) Participation in one or more acts of copulation.
(4) Pregnancy.
(5) Childbirth.

In essence, it does not matter if a woman is rude, crude, filthy, illiterate, retarded, or just plain stupid if she can acquire enough sperm through her vaginal canal to become pregnant and give birth to a child, the state will support her as the person apprently most qualified to rear the child. And if the child grows up to be a delinquent as so many do, some theorize that such delinquency could have been avoided if we had provided the mother with more money; or perhaps if welfare regulations were

179

revised we could keep the woman's would-be-husband or lover in the home and thus many children could benefit by the expert child rearing practices of what most people call bums, the police call "scum" but what many academicians call parents who should be in the home influencing the children they sired. The point to be made is that keeping the family together is not the answer. In fact I would argue that keeping the family together is the antithesis of the answer.

We should not let policy be guided by the assumption of competence. Simply because a man and a woman are competent enough to engage in intercourse, we should not assume competence in the area of child rearing. In fact, I believe it would be reasonable to assume that a parent or parents are incomptent if they cannot feed, clothe, house, and supervise their child or children without welfare assistance.

Obviously, there are a large number of parents who should not be allowed to rear children. A legislative committee of the Illnois House of Representatives reported in 1977 (Southern Illinoian, 2-2-77) that more than 30,000 children are victims of sexual abuse every year in Illinois.

The study showed that intrafamily sexual abuse of children occurs three times as often as incidents involving molestation by strangers. Incestuous relationships, generally between father and daughter or stepfather and stepdaughter, pose the largest problems, the study said.

Often the mother is aware of the situation and . . . refuses to acknowledge it, either because she fears her husband, is dependent upon him for financial support, or because she is relieved to shift the burden of an unwanted physical relationship to someone else, the report said.

Judicial proceedings against offenders often are hampered, the study said, because many times young children don't qualify as witnesses due to their age.

Another problem is that police, state's attorneys or judges often lack interest in child abuse cases because convictions are hard to gain, the report added.

180

The report said, however, that many of the runaways 'flee parents, siblings or guardians who beat them or use them in sexual activities.' Returning them to their family environment is not always the best solution, the report said.

Reports about child abuse are not hard to find. On July 2, 1978, a story appeared in the Austin American-Statesman entitled "Father of Caged Kids Says He Wants Children Back"

James (Chief) Williston says he wants back his three children county welfare officials took away because they found them naked, covered with dirt and excrement and penned in a chicken-wire cage behind his shack.

The children range in age from 1 to 2.

'I had them back in the pen. I made me a little old pen to keep the babies in, so they wouldn't get out on the highway,' said Williston, 57, a Choctaw who says he has two wives, both retarded, and four other children living at home.

Williston said his two previous wives — those were monogamous marriages, he said — both died. He had a total of five children by them, all grown and now living on their own.

If I could get hold of the Indian nation in Idabel (Oklahoma), it would be all right, but I can't do that. I don't know what to do. I want to get my babies back, he said Friday in an interview.

Bowie County Sheriff Earl Sabo said the pen was about 6 feet by 6 feet, and about 3 feet high. 'Just tall enough for them to stand in,' Sabo said.

Williston said his two wives, age 22 and age 20, are sisters.

'They're mentally retarded, both of 'em, and I take care of 'em. They do all right. They can cook, take care of the babies. And they are pretty good for digging potatoes. We manage,' he said.

Both women (his wives) are reportedly 5 months pregnant.

181

More severe cases of child abuse are reported daily in city newspapers across the nation. For example, on January 14, 1979, the Austin American-Statesman carried a story about two children battered by their mother.

Police found the children in their blood-spattered, litter-strewn apartment Friday.

One of them, Clifford Cecil Grandi, 11, had a screwdriver imbedded to the hilt through his right eye and screamed when officers found him hiding beneath the stairs.

His 8 year-old stepsister, Aimee Jean Gray, had been beaten and stabbed, and her skull was fractured. She was found unconscious near the front door.

Both children remained hospitalized in critical condition late Saturday. The boy underwent two operations overnight at Dallas' Parkland Hospital. The girl underwent surgery at Baylor Medical Center in Dallas.

We are presently spending billions of tax dollars to subsidize incompetent parents. Thus, our present welfare orientation perpetuates behavioral problems as well as socially and educationally inadequate individuals.

I propose that family welfare assistance (e.g., aid to dependent children) be eliminated.* I further propose that the different states use those same welfare tax dollars to construct, staff, and maintain numerous child-rearing-educational-institutions. The proposed child-rearing-educational-institutions should be designed to rear children from birth through high school. The very best educational technology and behavioral expertise available should be utilized to prepare a structured environment which would be most beneficial for the children as well as society in general. By removing children from the home of parents incapable of rearing them we can offer those same children the best our society has to offer. We can construct the ideal environment, prevent the development of anti-social and criminal behavioral patterns, and offer the highest quality academic and vocational

---

*This is not to say that exceptional cases would not be recognized. For example, an extremely competent parent suffering temporary physical impairment might receive family welfare assistance.

education available. Strictly supervised child-rearing-educational-institutions making full use of the very best educational and behavioral expertise available would undoubtedly achieve a position of scholastic, vocational, and athletic superiority when compared to traditional educational systems operating in the United States today.

VIII
Recommendations For
Control

Martin R. Haskell and Lewis Yablonsky (1978:549-550) argue that community treatment facilities should be expanded. They point out that there is considerable evidence to support the assertion that placing people in custody often serves to reinforce patterns of criminal behavior. "If people are not yet committed to criminal or delinquent attitudes and values when they enter a correctional institution, they are likely to learn them there. Those who arrive with few criminal skills often acquire them before they leave (1978:549)." Therefore, Haskell and Yablonsky feel that all offenders should be treated in the community unless they absolutely require custody. "In brief, we recommend increased support and establishment of community-based programs in lieu of confinement in custodial institutions. Confinement in a total institution would be ordered only in those instances where it was clearly necessary to protect society or where all other treatment efforts had failed (1978:550)."

I would not disagree with Haskell and Yablonsky when they argue that people sentenced to correctional institutions are likely to learn criminal or delinquent attitudes. However, I do not believe that correctional facilities have to be crime schools. Obviously, they do not. Correctional facilities can be devised to eliminate the crime school environment.

I personally feel that to emphasize community-based programs in lieu of confinement as advocated by Haskell and Yablonsky and others is in error. At a time when young offenders are committing violent acts and stealing with awesome regularity our criminal justice system seems to pride itself on laxity in the form of nominal punishment and community based programs. By emphasizing rehabilitative community based programs, and attempting to eliminate the stigma as well as inconveniences of incarceration, we are in danger of subsidizing criminal behavior. We are approaching the point where being admitted to our correctional system may be preferable to the present life situation of millions of people living in the United States today. When this occurs we have created and encouraged anarchy for the disadvantaged. When young offenders are no longer punished but enrolled in rehabilitative programs designed not to punish but to assist them in developing academic and vocational skills we should not be surprised at increased criminal behavior.

Let me illustrate the point. During the fall semester of 1976, I was employed as a half-time lecturer at Southern Illinois University. I was one of the more fortunate Ph.D. students in residence. I received a half-time faculty appointment with the accompanying salary of $550.00 per month. Other Ph.D. students not fortunate enough to be appointed as half-time lecturers were employed as teaching assistants at $320 to $350 per month, or worked menial jobs in the City of Carbondale. Ph.D. students in the Psychology Department who were fortunate enough to receive teaching assistantships also received between $320 and $350 per month or worked whatever jobs were available in the city to support themselves while they pursued a Ph.D. Needless to say, if a part-time counseling position had been advertised at the starting salary of $500.00 per month, Ph.D. students in Sociology and Psychology would have jumped at the chance to acquire such employment. However, a twenty year old junior majoring in social welfare held the posi-

186

tion. He worked as a counselor at the Synergy Crisis Information Center in Carbondale, located next to the University. How did this young man acquire such an envied position? It's simple. He was being rehabilitated. He and 32 other offenders sentenced to prison terms were serving their time at a work release center in Carbondale.

> He paid the center $25.00 a week for room and board out of the $500.00 a month he earned at Synergy. That salary was paid with federal funds from the Comprehensive Employment Training Act.
>
> His tuition at SIU-C and other expenses were also paid for by the federal government through a Basic Opportunity Grant (Southern Illinoisan, 1-30-77).

This young offender had not acquired his favored position, his college scholarship, and additional governmental assistance because he was an underprivileged child. No! He acquired special attention, special programming, and a favored position in society because six year earlier at age 14 he killed his 12 year old sister and her 11 year old friend with a shotgun.

As the case related above demonstrates, many rehabilitation programs have become nonsensical. We have reached the point where offenders receive more attention and more assistance than do their law abiding peers. For example, in the state of Illinois every offender obtains a college scholarship, a small monthly salary, vocational instruction, and free counseling as well as other benefits when he is sentenced to a state correctional facility. In essence, we are rewarding those underprivileged individuals who commit serious criminal acts. Never has there been a better example of the old adage "the squeaky wheel gets the grease." We seem to be saying if an underprivileged individual chooses to abide by the law "that's his tough luck." If he chooses to violate the law, victimize the citizenry, and commit serious criminal acts we will offer him special attention and opportunities which would not have otherwise been made available. Unfortunately, the lunacy of such social policy is not obvious to all.

It is my contention that we need a realistic social policy to deal with offenders. The first priority of all rehabilitative efforts should be the law abiding underprivileged. We must stop penalizing the law abiding underprivileged for their lawful behavior at the same time we are rewarding the lawless.

We should emphasize rehabilitation for the law abiding underprivileged. We should emphasize control when dealing with the lawless. This is not to say that offenders sentenced to correctional facilities should not be provided with academic instruction, vocational training, and counseling. But in my view, an academic, vocational, or counseling program should not be made available to inmates until the same program is made available to the law abiding citizenry of our society. Let us begin to reward lawful behavior with subsidized academic, vocational, and counseling programs; and let us begin to penalize criminal behavior by making inmates secondary targets of our rehabilitative efforts.

TOWARD A CONTROLLED CORRECTIONAL SYSTEM

The first step in developing a controlled correctional system is compiling comprehensive criminal records beginning at the earliest possible point in an offender's life. Law enforcement and correctional personnel should concentrate on constructing comprehensive documented life histories of offenders in order to eliminate criminal careers by identifying and incarcerating offenders as early as possible.

GENERAL OUTLINE FOR A
CONTROLLED CORRECTIONAL SYSTEM

Obviously we should stop incarcerating juveniles for committing *status offenses*, i.e., those crimes that would not be criminal if committed by an adult. The following quote exemplifies the point very well:

As 16-year-old Mike walked along a city street after midnight, a police cruiser pulled up to the curb. After questioning, Mike was taken to a juvenile detention center, where records revealed he was a four-time violator of the city's 11 p.m. curfew ordinance. He was placed in a boys' training school until either he or his parents could control his behavior.

On the other hand, Larry, 15, was arrested when police caught him with stolen merchandise. The judge returned Larry to his parents' custody.

Or take Scott, 16, who argued constantly with his mother. After being in and out of court half a dozen times, the boy's mother asked the judge to remove him from her home. Scott has spent the last 18 months in a juvenile center.

Yet in New York recently, a judge sentenced a 15-year-old convicted murderer to just five years in prison. Moreover, in 18 months the boy can be transferred to a juvenile facility for the remainder of his sentence.

How can such disparity exist in the handling of youths who commit no crimes — like Mike and Scott — and those who do commit crimes? The answer lies in how they are classified under our justice system. Children who commit actual crimes, like Larry and the New York boy, are classified as "juvenile criminals" and entitled to due process of law. But children like Mike and Scott, termed "status offenders," lack such protection.

Juvenile criminals are children under 18 who have committed crimes against persons or property. Status offenders are children who have done things that would go unpunished if done by adults. These include truancy, running away, curfew violations, smoking, drinking, even arguing (Diegmueller, 1978:14).

Community based programs should be designed to deal with status offenders. Status offenders may be a nuisance, but they are not preying upon the citizenry of the community or victimizing their fellow man, thus incarceration is not warranted. It does not seem unreasonable to advocate the right of every individual to pursue whatever course of action they desire, if, and only if, such pursuance does not harm another individual physically or economically. However, those individuals who commit criminal acts which do harm others physically (criminal homicide, attempted murder, aggravated battery, rape, etc) or economically (armed robbery, robbery, burglary, fraud, theft, etc) should be dealt with in a stern and consistent manner.

Too frequently violent and/or predatory criminals are excused in large part because they are black, brown, poor, or reflect some other characteristic which may have been disadvantageous in their earlier development. This naive forgiving attitude may be viewed as virtuous by many, but such an attitude does not contribute to the maintenance of consistent behavioral standards in a society. In fact, such naive unrealistic attitudes prevent us from dealing sternly and consistently with those individuals who rob, beat, rape, and murder citizens in our communities daily.

The plain fact is that there are numerous individuals presently residing in our society who are stealing, robbing, burglarizing, beating, raping, and murdering other members of our society. Poor people are not the criminals. The obvious, although illusive truth, is that many poor people commit criminal acts, but most poor people are law abiding. It is extremely simpleminded, one might even say irresponsible, to talk about the lawfulness of poor people as though poor people are all alike. However, such portrayals of poor people in the United States are not difficult to find.

It seems as though many of us, particularly academicians, no longer talk about those who steal, rob, burglarize, beat, assault, rape, murder, etc., as contrasted to those who do not. Not infrequently, criminologists presently in vogue argue that manufacturers responsible for unsafe automobiles and air pollution are the real criminals, and our attention should be shifted away from street crime and toward white collar and industrial crime. Although law enforcement efforts in the area of industrial and white collar crime should be increased, such enforcement efforts should not detract from the goal of creating a safe society in which a citizen can not only breath fresh air and drive a safe car, but also a society in which people are not robbed, raped, beaten or murdered with the regularity which is the present norm in our society.

For too many years we have treated many of the most violent predatory offenders with laxity and naivete beyond rationality. We have repeatedly and irresponsibly excused the most violent and ruthless offenders as mentally ill or insane. Recently a clinical psychologist who co-authored a study on criminal motivation, based on 17 years of research at the government's St. Elizabeth's Hospital in Washington, reported that allowing insanity as a defense plea in criminal court is a charade.

'It is a charade participated in by the courts, some psychiatrists and criminals,' Dr. Stanton E. Samenow says.

Samenow was asked about his study in light of the scheduled sentencing Monday of David Berkowitz, New York City's 'Son of Sam' killer whose case has re-kindled debate in the legal and psychiatric profession: At what point should the court say that a defendant's mental condition relieves him of responsibility for a crime?

Samenow's findings challenge the long-standing principle under which criminals plead insanity as a defense in court.

The psychologist and his late research partner, psychiatrist Samuel Yochelson, shook up the field of criminology last year with the publication of the first two volumes of their massive study, 'The Criminal Personality.'

The study attacks the theory that criminals are the product of deprived social conditions. It holds that criminals suffer from deviant thinking patterns. Samenow and Yochelson said confirmed criminals are able to block out inhibitions and convince themselves that every action they take is 'good' no matter what harm is done to others.

The researchers conducted 8,000 hours of interviews, with 255 male criminals, including killers, many of whom had been referred by courts to St. Elizabeth's because they pleaded not guilty by reason of insanity.

Samenow said the research team never found one person who was so out of touch with reality that he did

191

not know what he was doing when he committed the crime.

'If a person commits a felony and faces a conviction,' Samenow said, 'there is a lore in the District of Columbia, in the streets and among lawyers that if you can convince a court and a psychiatrist that you're insane, you go to a hospital and not to prison.'

'In the hospital, the conditions are better. If you play the psychiatric game, you can get out sooner and beat the charge.'

For each of the criminals in the study group, these questions about their acts were explored in detail: Was his action purposeful and deliberate? Was the criminal in control of his behavior? Was he in touch with reality?

'In every one of these cases, the answer to all the questions was yes,' Samenow said (Austin American Statesman, 6-11-78).

Some kids are just bad. They lie and cheat and skip school; they try to bully their parents, rejecting love if it is offered. When these children grow up, they rob, embezzle, rape and kill. Crime turns them on. The doctors conclude that, for unknown reasons, hardcore criminals simply choose, from early childhood, to engage in antisocial behavior.

The Washington study has stirred controversy among criminologists because it challenges nearly all conventional modern doctrine.

Most authorities have long contended that criminals are usually products of bad homes, poverty and discrimination, or else are mentally ill. Yochelson, who died last summer after spending sixteen years on the project, and Samenow dismiss most of both theories. Many of the criminals they examined came from law-abiding families; and although the criminals had often been treated as psychotic, the diagnosis later proved unreliable. The doctors, also found no genetic pattern — no 'bad seed.' In short, after perhaps the most detailed study of the hard-core criminal ever attempted, they have isolated a consistent profile of behavior — but they do not claim to have found a cause.

As they perceive it, hard-core criminality knows no economic or racial distinctions. Criminal whites from suburban backgrounds and blacks from the inner city have more in common with each other than they do with law-abiding members of their own races (no women were in the study, but Samenow speculates that women would prove no different). Nor does it matter much what kinds of crimes the men commit. 'The con artist views violence as crude, while the street criminal views the swindler as a sissy,' says Samenow, 'but if we look at their views of themselves, there are far more similarities than differences.'

The criminals' traits form a compendium of incivility: they are lying, evasive, manipulative, paranoid, cunning and secretive. A responsible person may lie occasionally, but for the criminal, 'lying comes as naturally as breathing,' says Samenow. 'If he is going to the grocery store, he will say it's the Safeway even if he intends to go to Grand Union.' The hard-core criminal spends enormous amounts of time just pondering crimes he could not possibly commit. 'Thinking about a crime is itself exciting,' write the authors. If the criminal walks into a store to buy cigarettes, he will calculate whether he could clean out the cash register or violate the women. Criminals do not behave impulsively. 'If the risks are too great, he does not act,' the study says. But the criminal is also 'super-optimistic,' and when he does attempt a crime, he never expects to get caught.

. . . corrections officials tend to recognize the conclusions in their own experience. Says George Horvat, chief of psychological services at the U.S. Terminal Island prison in California: 'Most psychologists working here find this one of the most accurate descriptions of the criminal personality they have ever seen (Newsweek, 1978:91).'

The plain truth is that behavioral scientists (Sociologists, Psychiatrists, Psychologists) do not know much about the causes of criminal behavior. However, the mass media and many behavioral scientists have deceived legislatures and the general public; thus many people feel behavioral scientists can actually cure (change) behavioral patterns through counseling.

It is my contention that behavioral scientists could better assist society if we (behavioral scientists) would emphasize honesty over self aggrandizement. Since the best behavioral technology (Skinnerian-Behavioralism) presently available is at odds with our legal system, perhaps we should emphasize control until we have developed methods of changing behavior which do not infringe on the constitutional rights of offenders.*

Most recently we have tried a kind of hockey-style penalty-box corrections approach which has proved to be ineffectual as well as dangerous in that it allows the repeated victimization of the citizenry by convicted offenders. This penalty-box corrections approach consists of rounding up offenders, incarcerating them for short periods of time,** releasing them, and then attempting to round them up again for another short stay in the penalty-box.

Presently there are approximately 300,000 people incarcerated in the United States. The vast majority will be released within the next few years. The majority of those released will continue to prey upon the citizenry as before, and will continue such behavior until they are apprehended and returned to prison. Obviously, short term incarceration does not protect society or deter potential offenders.

If our goal is to create a society in which people are not robbed, raped, beaten, or murdered, we should busy ourselves

---

*The other alternative involves changing the Federal as well as State Constitutions in order to eliminate the constitutional rights of convicted offenders which prevent the use of Skinnerian-Behavioralism.

**Although many states deceive the public by sentencing offenders to serve many years in penitentiaries, in reality only a small fraction of the time is ever served as evidenced by the case histories cited in Chapters IV and V.

with the task of identifying and removing from society those who commit violent and/or predatory offenses. We must also accept the financial burden. If we want safer communities we must be willing to spend the needed money. If we decide to stop using the short term penalty-box approach, prison populations will increase. We must be willing to finance the incarceration of 1% (2.5 million) of the population if need be.

If we want safer streets we can have them. If we are tired of reading about former offenders robbing, raping, or murdering again and again, we can eliminate opportunities for the would-be repeat offenders. The answer is obvious; extend the minimum period of incarceration for violent and/or predatory offenders.

TOWARD A CONTROLLED PRISON SYSTEM

Although it is frequently assumed that the more violent offenders and repeat offenders suffer the most and are placed in the most strictly supervised and least desirable correctional institutions, this is not always the case. In large penitentiaries the usual procedure is as follows: The more serious offenders occupy the most prestigious positions, the best prison jobs, and the best living quarters. Serious offenders frequently exercise power over the lives of other inmates because with the passage of time they become very familiar to the prison guards, and they frequently assist the guards in the repetitive day-to-day operations of the prison. Therefore, a large number of serious offenders are generally viewed by members of the prison staff as "good-ole-boys" warranting a measure of trust and responsibility. Not surprisingly prison organizations and gangs which prey on the general inmate population are controlled and operated by the more serious offenders.

The plight of first timers and marginal offenders in the prison environment is a hard one. Upon admission to the prison environment the less predatory, less violent offenders are victimized by the more violent, more predatory offenders.

Obviously we need to institute strict supervision and meaningful security levels in order to assure some measure of justice in our correctional institutions. Although virtually all states have different security levels ranging from minimum security or trusty status to maximum security, in reality the distinctions are frequently more clerical than real, and offenders with different security classifications are mixed together and not infrequently are housed together. This practice contributes to the victimization of the less violent by the more violent and allows inmates to live by the same code which society condemns, that is, the strong (most violent and predatory) do as they please, the weak are victimized.

To alleviate the crime school environment and inmate brutality which plagues most large penitentiaries, a system of institutions, each with a single security level should be designed. However, all institutions should emphasize extremely strict supervision and discipline.

AMNESTY UPON COMPLETION OF SENTENCE?

Many have argued for amnesty upon completion of sentence. Haskell and Yablonsky (1978:557) assert that when an offender — adolescent or adult — completes his sentence whether in an institution or on probation or parole, he should be considered to have "paid his debt to society." Obviously, arrest and conviction records handicap an individual when he seeks legitimate employment. However, I would argue that an ex-offender should be handicapped. Rather than bemoaning the fact that ex-offenders may be denied local licenses and security clearances, I would argue that ex-offenders should be discriminated against. There is no such thing as "paying one's debt to society." When a man serves his time and walks out of prison, he hasn't "paid his debt to society." He has simply completed a period of incarceration which he was ordered to serve because of crimes committed against one or more members of the community. We "pay our debt to society" when we pay income tax. When a man walks out of prison after serving 15 years for using an 8 year old girl's throat as if it was a vagina (which caused the girl's death by suffocation) he has not "paid his debt to society." There is no debt to be paid to society. The plain fact is the man is a dangerous sex offender and if the powers that rule in our society allow the release of such offenders, we should not sit around saying "I'm okay, You're okay," "you've paid your debt to society." In my view the

196

man should be treated as a potentially dangerous child molester and not allowed to work in or near children's homes, grade schools, etc.

I use the example of a child molester because during my tenure as a correctional sociologist at Mid-State Penitentiary, I was interviewing a child molester one day and I asked him what he wanted to do when released from the penitentiary. He commented, "I want to work with children." I remember thinking to myself "yes, he probably will get a job working with children." Unfortunately, many behavioral scientists such as Haskell and Yablonsky (1978:558) insist that arrest and conviction records must be removed from public availability in order to give ex-offenders a new start. I respectfully disagree. I am a firm believer that an individual should be viewed in light of his past behavior. An habitual thief should be dealt with as an habitual thief and the only way to determine habituation is through access to carefully prepared and comprehensive criminal records beginning at the earliest possible point in an offender's life. I am not convinced of the advantages procured by expunging juvenile records or blocking access to criminal records. However, the advantages derived by offenders is quite obvious.

Bibliography

Austin American-Statesman
    1978-79 Austin, Texas.

Cleaver, Eldridge
    1969 Post-Prison Writings and Speeches. New York: A Ramparts Book by Random House.

Diegmueller, Karen
    1978 "The Forgotton Juveniles: 'Crim-Les' Criminals." Parade, September 3, 14-15.

Federal Bureau of Investigation, U.S. Department of Justice
    1977 Uniform Crime Reports for the United States, 1976. Washington, D.C.: U.S. Government Printing Office.

Frazier, Charles E.
    1978 "The Use of Life-Histories in Testing Theories of Criminal Behavior: Toward Reviving a Method." Qualitative Sociology 1 (May): 122-142.

Gordon, David M.
    1975 "Class and the Economics of Crime," in W. J. Chambliss (ed.) Criminal Law in Action. Santa Barbara, California: Hamilton Publishing.

Griffin, Susan
 1975 "Rape: The All-American Crime," in W. J. Chambliss (ed.) Criminal Law in Action. Santa Barbara, California: Hamilton Publishing.

Haskell, Martin R. and Lewis Yablonsky
 1978 Juvenile Delinquency. Chicago: Rand McNally.

Jackson, George
 1970 Soledad Brothers, New York: Bantam Books.

Newsweek
 1978 "The Criminal Mind." Feb. 27, Vol. XCL, No. 9.

President's Commission
 1968 The Challenge of Crime in a Free Society: The President's Commission on Law Enforcement and Administration of Justice. New York: Avon Books.

Roebuck, Julian B.
 1978 "Where Do We Go From Here?" Sociological Forum 1: 83-86.

Shaw, Clifford R.
 1930 The Jack-Roller. Chicago: University of Chicago Press.

Shaw, Clifford R.
 1931 The Natural History of a Delinquent Career. Chicago: University of Chicago Press.

Shaw, Clifford R., H. David McKay, and J. F. McDonald
 1938 Brothers in Crime. Chicago: University of Chicago Press.

Skinner, B. F.
 1971 Beyond Freedom and Dignity. New York: Alfred A. Knopf.

Southern Illinoisan
1977 Carbondale, Illinois.

Southerland, Edwin
1937 The Professional Thief. Chicago: University of Chicago Press.

Thomas, W. I.
1909 Source Book for Social Origins. Chicago: University of Chicago Press.

Thomas, W. I. and Florian Znaniecki
1927 The Polish Peasant in Europe and America. Vol. 2 New York: Alfred A. Knapf.

Thomas, W. I. and Dorothy Swain Thomas
1928 The Child in America. New York: Alfred A. Knopf.

Yochelson, Samuel and Stanton E. Samenow
1976 The Criminal Personality Volume I: A Profile for Change. New York: Jason Aronson.

Yochelson, Samuel and Stanton E. Samenow
1977 The Criminal Personality Volume II: The Change Process. New York: Jason Aronson.